Blessed With Unusual Happiness

A Mother's Love Story About The Gift Of Diabetes
And So Much More

Ann Clute

Blessed With Unusual Happiness---©Copyright 2012
ISBN 147830930X
ISBN 9781478309307

By Ann M. Clute

For information: Ann Clute, Box 673, Hawley, MN 56549
AnnCluteFaithLife@gmail.com

First Edition

Cover Design by Kathy Anderson

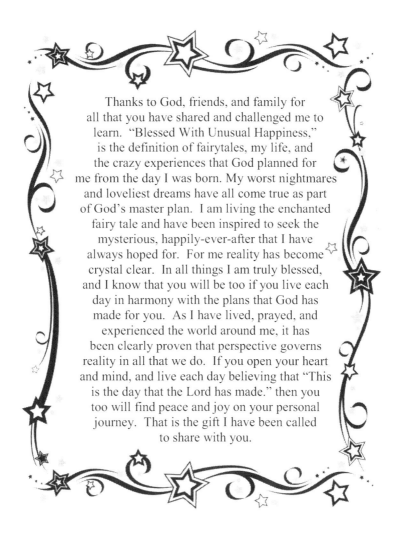

Thanks to God, friends, and family for
all that you have shared and challenged me to
learn. "Blessed With Unusual Happiness,"
is the definition of fairytales, my life, and
the crazy experiences that God planned for
me from the day I was born. My worst nightmares
and loveliest dreams have all come true as part
of God's master plan. I am living the enchanted
fairy tale and have been inspired to seek the
mysterious, happily-ever-after that I have
always hoped for. For me reality has become
crystal clear. In all things I am truly blessed,
and I know that you will be too if you live each
day in harmony with the plans that God has
made for you. As I have lived, prayed, and
experienced the world around me, it has
been clearly proven that perspective governs
reality in all that we do. If you open your heart
and mind, and live each day believing that "This
is the day that the Lord has made." then you
too will find peace and joy on your personal
journey. That is the gift I have been called
to share with you.

Contents

Introduction

This is not a simple story. This is not a fiction novel. This is a true fairy tale. "Blessed With Unusual Happiness" is about real life and real people with real love, real faith, and real determination to beat unreal odds. Before I began writing, I wanted to make sure that this story is really unique and valuable. I did a lot of research and used the information I found to justify that my story is mathematically unique. I am not a mathematician, so please forgive me if my calculations are not perfect but the facts and circumstances of my life and the ways the blessings have unfolded make it clear that this is a unique story. There are three people with type 1 diabetes in our unusual family of seven people. The odds are 2.3 in 1 trillion that three people aged 3, 4, and 11 would all become type 1 diabetics in the same family. The numbers allow me to say that what I have lived is highly unlikely. I know unquestionably that God led me to this place through His specific plan for me. My story is not an accident. It has to be an intentional act, by God, to show His power in helping people triumph in life despite adversity. It is unique and yet common because we all are challenged by health problems, financial challenges, stress, time management, etc., etc. Prayer, discussion, and self-reflection led me to write a story in order to help others cope with challenges … successfully. I guarantee that the stories, insights, emotions, and answers written here are valuable because they come from the wisdom and passion gathered faithfully from an investment of more than twenty-seven years of my life.

Erma Bombeck wrote a short piece on diabetes that inspired me to write this book. As most of you may know, she was an American humorist who achieved great popularity for her newspaper columns. She made a living telling interesting stories about ordinary suburban home life. One day, by accident, I came across a column written by her and titled "How God Selects the Mother of a Diabetic Child." For many reasons I hung onto the article. Over the months since I read it I have been hearing voices in my head that keep telling me to write this book. Because this little story has been an inspiration to me, it seems that sharing it is a perfect way to start this book.

"Most women become mothers by accident, some by choice, a few by social pressures and a couple by habit. Did you ever wonder how mothers of diabetics are chosen? Somehow, I visualize God hovering over Earth selecting his instruments for propagation with great care and deliberation. As he observes, he instructs his angels to make notes in a giant ledger.

"Armstrong, Beth, son. Patron Saint Matthew. "Forrest, Marge, daughter, Patron Saint Cecilia. Rutledge, Carrie, twins. Patron Saint Gerard He's used to profanity.

Finally, He passes a name to an angel and smiles. "Give her a child with diabetes." The angel is curious. "Why this one God? She is so happy."

"Exactly" Smiles God, "Could I give a child with diabetes to a mother who does not know laughter? That would be cruel."

"But has she the patience?" asks the angel.

"I don't want her to have too much patience, or she will drown in a sea of self-pity and despair. Once the shock and resentment wear off, she'll; handle it. I watched her today. She has that feeling of self and independence that is so rare and so necessary in a mother. You see, the child I am going to give her has her own world. She has to make it live in her world and that's not going to be easy.

"But Lord, I don't think she even believes in you."

God smiles, "No matter. I can fix that. This one is perfect she has just enough selfishness."

The angel gasps, "Selfishness? Is that a virtue?"

God nods. "If she cannot separate herself from the child occasionally, she will never survive. Yes, here is a woman whom I will bless with less than perfect."

"She does not realize it yet, but she is to be envied. I will permit her to see clearly the things I see... ignorance, cruelty, prejudice..., and allow her to rise above them. She will never be alone. I will be at her side every minute of every day of her life because she is doing my work as surely as if she is here by my side."

"And what about her patron saint?" asks the angel, his pen poised in midair.

God smiles, "A mirror will suffice."''

I am a very normal person but the story of my life seems in many ways special. I do not claim to have special medical, intellectual, or administrative insight but I really can share stories in a fun and positive way so that you might be inspired by something that you can use in your own life. I want mom's to know that they are never alone and that if they do their best, believe in God's will, and stay positive both they and their families can experience "unusual happiness."

Chapter One

For as long as I can remember, I always wanted to be a mom, not just a mom, but a really great mom. I was born as a baby boomer in 1959 to two parents whose lives could have been pulled right out of any classic movie storyline from the 50's. Back then everyone wanted to have a home like the neighbors, a solid job in the suburbs, and a way to contribute to life in their community. In high school, my mom was a popular cheerleader and my dad was the star four-sport athlete with quite a list of accomplishments and admirers. They met and began dating in Jr. High and stayed together until they both passed away within three months of one another. Like many parents they were the perfect couple and they lived a "perfect life".

Their perfection pressured me because they were royalty and they ruled my magical kingdom. As a result, my childhood came right out of a classic fairy tale like the ones that I loved to read. It was the perfect world. Good and bad were clearly defined. I knew that difficulty is normal and that it often leads to a whole bunch of real magic, a magnificent solution, and at the end there is a happy ending. That is the life I lived and expected. That is what I was determined to have. It was the vision for my happily ever after.

I always trusted and believed that everything is good. Worry is a waste of time. I always looked forward to something magical. It was a feeling. It was a spirit. It was energy. It kept me believing that something truly spectacular would happen today or tomorrow. My story was "Snow White" because she was angelic in every way. She was not from any place special. She didn't have any qualifications. She was simply beautiful on the outside and the inside. The world adored her because of her kindness, wisdom, and patience. These were the qualities I wanted. This story was my calling in life.

I always cared about everyone. I wanted to understand people's strengths, weaknesses, needs, and wants. I always loved younger people and wanted to share the same love and comfort that I felt at all times and in all places. My calling in life was to become a teacher and care giver. It was the earliest message that I heard from God. Jesus said, "Let the children come to me. Don't stop them! The Kingdom of Heaven belongs to those who are like these children." That was my destiny.

When I graduated from high school, I decided to attend the same small Lutheran College in Minnesota where my perfect parents' perfect life together had begun. I still wanted to become a real princess and live the perfect life but I also wanted to learn more about who God wanted me to be. In the time when drinking, drugs, parties, and fast cars were all a compelling pressure and legal even for 18-year-old kids I was learning about something more important. Much of my education was about passion and love. The passion came from incredible friendships and experiences that happened. The love that I found was in living my dream to teach children and become a perfect mother for the babies that I planned to have. When I graduated with my elementary degree I was ready to face the real world head on.

Unlike mom and dad, the prince charming that I expected to see riding in on a white horse between those college dorms or down the aisle in the library did not show up. I needed to learn to overcome obstacles myself, to be an independent thinker and doer, and finally to remain true to my purposes and values. I was being prepared for what would be an incredible next step on my journey. Every day when I arose to live, it happened with the belief in my heart, and mind that somewhere, somehow I would meet the right man to live with "happily ever after".

Chapter Two

ecause I wasn't yet riding into the sunrise of my future with my prince charming, I needed to find a job and begin by myself. I searched for the perfect place at this perfect time. I was thrilled when I landed my first teaching position, got my first contract, and decorated my first grade room. When I started, I immediately loved the look in the children's eyes. I loved to answer their questions. I could not wait to hear their voices when they came into my room in the morning. I felt their love as I encouraged them and shared with them as they pursued the same dreams and expectations that I had just a few short years ago.

I loved the children, but I am certainly intelligent enough to know that I could not wait around for 20 years in order to marry one of them. Just joking, but this was my time and I could feel the desire, so it was also a time for me to keep my eyes open for Mr. Right. My first job in a little Minnesota town only lasted for one year. I probably would have stayed, but God had a different plan. The job that seemed so perfect did not last after that first year because it was cut from the budget. It was a sad day when I learned I would be leaving, but I am positive now that my prince would never have ridden his horse – more appropriately "64" Mustang convertible - into my world. I realized somewhere between my first, second, and third teaching jobs that I was not supposed to be out finding the perfect man for me, but instead, like in the fairy tales, I had to simply believe and it would come true. I left my dreamy expectations behind and placed what would become of me in God's hands. That is why it has all been so good despite the fact that it has never been what I would have once called perfect.

In my early adult life I suddenly learned to give up control and instead, give up to God. I learned that what would be is what is supposed to be. When I quit hoping, searching, and expecting, the future became the present and he, the man of my dreams, came to appear right out of the blue. That magical theme continues throughout my life. My advice for all things is that it is good to plan but it is better to pray faithfully and believe that you are where you are supposed. Then you can really see where you are and know what you should be planning for. My life has truly proven that if I believe in God's will and His powerful plans I am always where I am supposed to be. When I am in God's chosen place, the right things always happen.

It was an October night when my world began to change. My closest friend had traveled close to 400 miles to spend a couple of nights with me and we went out to one of the local dance clubs. As we were sitting, visiting, and enjoying the evening with the laughing, and crazy disco crowd, our fun was changed to focus when a handsome, blonde, very fit and funny young man came, sat down and began visiting as though we were lifelong friends. He was, in fact, a close friend of my girlfriend's brothers. His demeanor was unique from any that I had ever known. He simply seemed so relaxed, confident, and sincere that I could hardly believe that he was for real. He winked at me like no one before and peered into my eyes as though he could see right into my heart.

I was not sure what to think, but something unusual had happened. At closing time, he left with his friends but I could still feel something that I had never felt before. As my friend Mary and I were walking back to our car, she asked if I would like to get to know him better. I immediately said, "He just seems unbelievably happy, and is different from anyone else I have met."

Throughout the night, and into the next day I kept wondering, "Was he for real?" By 3 o'clock the next day with Mary encouraging me and standing at my side I broke all of the rules in my rulebook and called him to invite him over to watch a football game and have dinner with me. What is happening to me? Was this me or some spirit who is guiding me? What angel comes into your life who takes over so much power that you wonder what is going on? Psalm 23:6 describes it quite well "Surely goodness and love will follow me all the days of my life, and I will dwell in the house of the LORD forever."

My first night with this unusual young man named Steve was incredibly unique. I made my best pepperoni pizza with "Worms' N Dirt" desert – this had no spiritual plan behind it - and we did not stop talking until I invited him to watch the football game while I cleaned the dishes and kitchen up. He went and stretched out on my living room floor but never quit visiting about the most interesting parts of both of our lives. When I walked into my own living room to join him something really crazy happened and we still laugh about it today. I have been known to trip over my own feet and never thought it could happen on a first date. I am so embarrassed by my unusual clumsiness. In this case I lost my balance and fell right down on top of his chest. As you may expect, it was extremely embarrassing when I was trying so hard to impress him. He did not even flinch and looked like nothing new had really happened. He was so cool about everything and without a blink he simply pushed me up and said, "I normally have to ask girls to do that." It seemed that somewhere within him there was a sense of humor, calm, and confidence that was unusual and I wanted to know why and how he had that. We started dating and his energy and joy for life became an addiction for me. He was fun and his unreal positive attitude about life matched my enthusiasm for living.

He was the young manager of a very new and very recognized business called Gold's Gym. It was actually only the 13th Golds Gym in the world. His personality played strong through all of the things he did in life and I remember wondering where this came from until the night that I first met his parents. They were both educators and very passionate about their professions. That set a very common ground for all of us. His easy smile and demeanor were obvious trademarks from both of his parents. There was also something in the way they all interacted that made it seem that there was something special in their love for one another. They all seemed perfect and I could not quite believe that my dream might really be happening. It seemed so unlikely but some voice inside me told me that I was going to the place that I had been looking for so long.

Believe it or not after about three months of dating I really tried to make it fall apart by telling him I was going on a blind date with another person. He responded by taking out a very attractive and really fun fitness trainer to go dancing. He proved that he was not desperate. I also tested Steve with my anger and bad moments. He was very unusual in his calm and patience and nothing that I did really seemed to irritate him. One time as I was suffering with my "time of the month" and would not answer the door because I did not want to see anyone. He simply climbed up the side of my apartment building from one balcony to the other all the way to the third floor and knocked on my deck window as I laid on the couch. He claimed that he was checking to make sure I was all right. He was hard to ignore. Things happened so easy and so comfortably and I know now that it was by God's plan. Obviously, my prince charming had finally arrived. Just like my favorite childhood fairy tales everything fit perfectly.

Our entire relationship was based upon easy laughter, unusual activities, sincerity, respect, honesty, and a shared faith in God. His world was filled with his faith, discipline, and desire for success. He was a complete leader and I loved being a part of who he was and where he was going. It seemed that there could be nothing that could make me doubt that I wanted to spend my life with Steve and then one day he asked me if I minded needles and people taking shots.

This is a question that I did not understand. Would you? I innocently asked him why and hoped that he was not a heroin addict, or dependent on steroids – how could I have missed that? Now seriously, the clumsiness and humility could certainly have been on him because this question was about for real and forever humility. He told me that he was a type 1 diabetic. He was quick to say that he had been living with this disease since he was three years old. He casually said that it is a disease with many possible complications but that he controlled it by being extremely active, watching his diet, and having fun in his life. His body was born with a problem that prevented him from having the insulin needed to keep his blood sugars regulated. In order to live and stay healthy he takes shots of something called insulin, which at that time was taken from pigs. This is no surprise now, because I always knew that he was not normal, he was unusual. Now I need to understand what I should feel, how I should act, what I should do about him and his relationship with me. He is one of the coolest people that I have ever known. God please help me to know the truth and the purpose of your will.

He told me that he could not live without insulin. He told me that he takes it every day and most likely would take it every day for the rest of his life. He told me that he overheard his doctor tell his mom outside his hospital room when he was diagnosed with the disease that he would probably live to enjoy 10-15 years of normal life. As his mother broke into tears, he told me that he had decided to prove that doctor wrong and to be as healthy and successful as anyone else in the world. He was only three when he made that decision. Another time he told me that he wanted to teach others how to care for themselves because he had done it every day of his life and felt very confident of the reasons for his success. Not knowing much about the disease, it really did not faze me much. I did not know any diabetics. He did not want me to be ignorant. He would not keep something this serious from me. He was a man of integrity and he was obviously testing my ability to approach and overcome the challenge just as he does every day.

Growing up, I knew my grandma had something similar, but just the opposite. She was hypoglycemic. I remember her getting up at night and being in the kitchen. The worst thing I remembered was overhearing a loud discussion late one night. My dad was reprimanding my grandma for being ornery and having a crappy attitude. My dad was frustrated, and was trying to pull my grandma out of her unusual disposition. It was confusing to me because it was the same grandma that I adored and thought was perfect. Looking back on that episode, the frustration displayed by my dad was purely ignorance in failing to understand the behaviors associated with her condition, which is one that I would grow to know only too well.

Steve seemed no different physically or mentally than anyone else I knew. He rarely talked about his disease. I think that not talking about it was his way of trying to spare me of the unnecessary worry that the disease involved. When I asked questions, he answered them honestly and concisely but he obviously did not act, think, or feel that diabetes had any negative impact on his life. I did not know until later, that up until he grew to love me, he thought that he would never be able to impose the risk and pain of his dealing with the disease on another person and especially not his wife. He thought that he would always remain single because of his desire not to make anyone else suffer because of his illness. In spite of his concerns, he always seemed to live like diabetes was a blessing to him rather than a curse. There is a different pressure for a person with diabetes to fall in love than a normal person. As I grew to understand, there are immense, proven risks that painful experiences related to suffering and death will come along with loving someone who lives with the disease.

He was always so much fun to be around and so in control of himself that I would forget all about him having the disease. The only time that the reality of diabetes in our world presented itself was in hypoglycemic incidences where he would grow pale, stubborn, far away and all of those who knew him, including me would hurry to find him a sugar drink, candy bar, or real food. His normal, rosy complexion would turn pale; his conversation would be altered by slurred speech and slight gibberish comments. It all appeared that he was becoming intoxicated but without the alcohol. I learned that the reality of diabetes was chemical and that these signs were simply early stages of his brain shutting down. He would sometimes get impatient and demanding, but I knew I had to stay calm and simply get some carbohydrates into him and sometimes very quickly. Once that was accomplished, I always knew that I would get my Stevie back and life was good again.

Because I loved him, I became more and more interested in diabetes and read about it and asked a lot of questions. Like much of the world of chemistry and biology it was confusing to me. I found it hard to understand all of the medical and scientific information. The devastating statistics and myriad of health problems that raise concern for and fear about the disease were overwhelming and scary. His answers to my questions were always satisfying and reassuring. His world was different than those who were trying to raise money for it and sell new drugs to treat the disease. Why would he believe that it would ruin his life. That is a sure way to let an illness control you. He has proven the theory that illness is to be feared wrong for many years. Instead of becoming afraid and running from him and his problem, I promised myself, just like he had, that I would not dwell on the negatives of the disease. I simply trust in my faith - the proven and real faith - that God has a plan for all of our lives and that he will watch over US and give me peace, grace, and guidance as I make huge decisions about my future.

After much prayer, consideration, wonderment, and distress I understood that this was meant to be. We moved forward with our relationship, staying extremely positive, energized, and passionate about the future and our life together. We both focused on the joy in each moment rather than on questions that no one would ever know if they did not live them. People with any chronic illness understand the requirements and live with those same ones every day. I loved him and truly knew that no matter what happened, the time that I spent was with my prince charming and that the gems of those moments would be the foundation of my happily ever after. My fairy tale story was being written, one page at a time. Now I know the direction for my life, and my dream world with its mystical future looks bright. We got engaged in the spring and he picked the season for a reason. His parents were married in June and he told me that "spring is a time for new beginnings." It certainly was the time for ours.

uring our months of engagement, Steve was living with his brother and wife. As I said before, life is not always easy for any of us. He had searched for jobs after attending law school and working for a year on his MBA but in 1983 those jobs were not easy to come by. He had worked for a year as an entrepreneur helping his brother launch a recording studio. Then he began working independently as a personal trainer and strength trainer for a world famous gymnastics program. Finally, he had entrepreneured his way into a general management position in the first health club in the region. His goal was to make the whole world healthy by being an example, mentor, motivator, and friend to everyone. Maybe he was a little driven to prove that diabetes was certainly not a physical limitation. He would do things like workout for two hours at 5:30 am then again at 9 pm. I watched him squat over seven hundred pounds. No matter how hard he worked or how much stress he endured he never grew tired.

The only scary times in our relationship grew from my experience with his disease. Once he got really sick with the flu. I wanted to make sure that nothing bad happened. I knew that sleep is important and that he needed to stay hydrated. Being present in case he needed anything seemed easy. I just did not know if a regular illness like the flu was different for someone with diabetes. How would I get him to eat or drink it if he was throwing up or sleeping? I did not want to keep waking him up all the time. Because sleep was essential when combating these flu symptoms, I had to stay on my toes to be aware of his state of mind. He did not own a glucometer - the medical device that measures the amount of sugar in the blood. It enables people with diabetes to monitor and take actions needed to properly manage the illness. He manages his illness strictly based upon how he is feeling - his learned sixth sense. Being Steve's nurse presented some challenges. I decided that I would purchase a meter to lower the chances of both long and short term complications. For my own comfort I woke him regularly to make sure he was breathing and then I would get him to talk or move around, to reassure me that he was all right. I quickly learned that when he broke into a sweat he was in need of carbohydrates and he recovered rapidly meaning that we made it through the first challenge. As my experience grew, I became more confident and comfortable just like he always was that he was not going to die from diabetic coma, or worse, die unnecessarily right there in front of me.

This was the first time I had seen my knight in shining armor as having a weakness. Making him well was my only priority. Selfish ways disappeared. He was so healthy and in control of his world. Now I shared control and his well-being was in my hands. For the first time, I knew that I would need to be his rock just as he was always mine. Diabetes is an illness that can be completely unnoticed and then suddenly and silently it changes a person's world. I felt empowered and somewhat overwhelmed by the responsibility for assuring that in both his strength and weakness he remained safe. (Just as in the classic fairy tale "Sleeping Beauty," an evil spell could cause him to fall into a deep sleep and only the kiss from his true love would waken him.) My love and care would forevermore serve to avoid any wicked spell.

Diabetes is a dilemma, but I never thought of it as a burden. I was prepared to make the most real promise in my world to him. In front of God and all who love us I would promise "to love him in sickness and health until death do us part." Finally, I had found my one true love, and my loveliest dreams would come true. Not diabetes, doubt, fear, disasters, or anything could stop us. I was not alone anymore. Obstacles are opportunities in disguise and God had set this first one in front and behind me very unexpectedly and suddenly. I was ready for the adventure. It is beyond my wildest dreams and it was beginning now!

We married at Christmas time. God might have been preparing us for something because two things happened. First, at our pastor's request we met privately with him an hour before our wedding rehearsal. This was the first time I was confronted with challenges about my decision to marry a person with diabetes. The pastor said it would be hard, with many sad moments and challenges, and that it may not be right for us. He left us with a recommendation to think very hard right now about what we were about to do. This does not seem to be a normal protocol for wedding counsel. Here it was, an hour immediately before our wedding rehearsal! I guess God was making it clear that this was meant to be. It would be very difficult to leave now. The talk obviously did not change anything but it did make me wonder where all of the pastor's concerns had all come from after us visiting weekly for five weeks leading up to this day. Maybe he just learned about Steve's illness. I wished he would have understood that I had thought long and hard about my decision to live my life with Steve . I knew he had a disease called diabetes but that didn't matter because my love for him was real and I understood that our time together was a gift, no matter how long that would be. How many people really faced these realities before they entered into a lifelong relationship? It certainly made me conscious and it certainly made me appreciative. I was truly blessed! Maybe if the pastor knew my preparedness he would have lessened his last minute warning. I guess a devil's advocate is not always a bad thing. He made me think, but he could not change my mind or my feelings.

Chapter Four

Steve was a gym owner and what you would call a "health nut." He became very health conscious as a young boy with diabetes. He was diagnosed back in 1959 at the age of three. His mother looks back on his diagnosis and associates it with a case of German measles he had when he was very young. She knew of no family members with the disease and struggled for answers to why he got diabetes. Scientists say that the cells can be destroyed by an autoimmune attack possibly as the result of a virus. Now there are many possible causes, but Steve never cares much about those. He says that blame is the same as going nowhere. He always says that he is going to stay healthy until they find a cure. Steve also reminds all of us when we hear hopeful news of cures that he has been hearing that there is a cure on the horizon ever since the early 60's. He follows by saying, "It's alright because it will just keep me alive well into my hundreds at the rate they are going." Is that staying positive or what?

His mother says that as a youngster he went to his doctor appointments every three months, just like clockwork. He grew up in a rural community, so going to a faraway land for these check-ups was always treated as an adventure. Steve's brother would go along and they would stay at a motel and eat out at a restaurant for breakfast as a reward for positive results. Steve did not like eating at restaurants as a young boy. He did not like restaurant food. Breakfast was good though because he liked pancakes and eggs. For him, Mom's carefully planned meals comprised of fresh vegetables, fruits, and home grown beef could not be equalled and were likely the reason for his good habits as well as his wonderful health today. Each check-up for him was like a mini-vacation. They always made this stressful event fun for Steve and they worked to make it a special outing for his brother, Michael, as well. They never wanted to show any favoritism. They wanted to treat the boys fairly and with equal attention, but they all knew that the disease had a power of its own. In conversations with Michael, he said that he always sort of felt like his mom worried and doted upon Steve. I am sure she did not want to show it, but Michael felt it. Today though, their love and respect for each other is incredibly obvious so in the end it was very well handled by everyone. Steve will not say much about how he felt about check-ups but he will admit that he did not like the get aways until the check-up and results were finished.

In the early 1960's there was no Humalog to immediately treat high blood glucose readings. There were no glucometers to know at all times if your blood sugar levels were correct. Diabetes was managed by habits – good habits. Drugs were relatively simple and much personal spontaneous treatment and decisions were based upon guesswork. Steve learned young that exercise was a good and painless way to keep his body feeling good and his blood sugars down and controlled. He tells a story of a night before a check-up when he had an opportunity to go to a birthday party for one of his friends. Of course, at a birthday party leaving cake, cookies, and candy alone is nearly impossible. Steve knew when he came home that he was going to get in trouble from his doctor. Before they left for their night at the hotel he went out to play basketball in order to forget about his worries. A couple of neighbors came over and they played late and right up until he had to leave for the motel. The next day, as he went in prepared to be reprimanded, he was surprised to hear the doctor say that all was perfect and to keep up the good work. That simple experience drove him to play and play and play anything and everything at all times and in all places. He became famous in town for being the only person around that would shoot baskets for hours upon hours in 40 mph winds and 50 below zero temperatures. He would even ride his bike around town while dribbling a basketball to get the most exercise possible at any one time. Steve's motivation was all God given and personally rewarding because it kept him feeling like a real athletic kid instead of a tired, achy, lethargic diabetic one.

Steve has lived his entire life on a mission to prove the doctors wrong. His mom, Delores, shared stories about his interesting background with diabetes. When he was only nine years old, his dad bought him a Charles Atlas weight set for Christmas. Why would you do that to a little kid? We know that it was a way for his dad to encourage him to be healthy. He was a quiet man but it was always easy to know that he felt great love and concern for his son. Even in the 60's, long before the time of commercialized fitness and nutrition, God was placing tools in his hands and encouraging him. Steve's intelligence and drive led him to intuitively grasp things that others would miss. He lifted, played, did push-ups, sit-ups, and chin-ups, and even hung a basketball hoop in his ugly dirt wall basement so the cold and rain would not stop him from being active and stronger than others at something that was physically demanding. As he grew older, Steve would lift weights in his garage and run every day. Delores also said that he always wanted to take vitamins and that he would always beg her for vitamin C. How could it be an accident that he did things that most children would not even think of?

It is interesting for me to think about the challenges Steve faced as a child with diabetes. He tells us that as a teenager at basketball practice, he remembers running lines until he could only see a white haze around him. He would finish practice and not remember how he got home. We will have to ask his legendary coach, Gene Manson, how he performed. Blood sugars were measured in those days by testing urine. The test results were not very accurate for an athlete with diabetes. In **www.Dr.com** it says, "A urine glucose test does not reflect your blood glucose level at the time of testing; instead, it gives an indication of your blood glucose level over the past several hours. For example, some of the urine present in your bladder may be two hours old, and may show glucose even though your blood glucose may have normalized since then. A urine glucose test does not give you any information about low blood glucose levels, as glucose is only found in the urine when the blood glucose level is above 10 mmol/L. That is, a negative urine glucose test may be the result of a normal blood glucose level or a dangerously low blood glucose level, with the urine glucose test unable to differentiate between the two situations." Steve says that he was physically aware of the inaccuracies because the way he felt would often not match the test numbers. He would simply have a candy bar or sweet drink when he was dizzy or could no longer see things clearly. (Back 100 years ago tasting the urine for sweetness was the only way to control it). Much has changed and as you will find out, I am "doubly blessed" that it has.

I do not mean to make it sound bad, but conditions for diabetes were so much different just thirty years ago. The disease is a plague and I think that much of it is due to ignorance, neglect, and lack of recognition of the innumerable ways that it affects anyone who lives it each day. The syringes that Steve used when we met were glass and so they were very fragile and not very efficient. Sterility was entirely dependent on keeping them immersed in alcohol and taking the time to boil them regularly. As a mom you would never know who had touched it, what it had touched or what potential risks occurred every day that you poked another injection into your child's arm, leg, stomach, or butt. Much of the education and management done to control the disease was based on diet. Eating habits and dietary restrictions were number one for good health in Steve's world. His mom was extremely committed to his well-being and she thought that candy and sweets were products of Satan when it came to his well-being. She went to serious lengths and made sure that all of the local grocery store and gas station attendants would not allow him to buy candy.

There are some very funny stories that he recalls pertaining to this. Independence in rural communities meant that kids often found ways to make money. For most, the celebration of a successful job outing was touring around the countryside happily on their bikes with a brown bag of penny candy. Steve remembers doing many things to enjoy the same savory treats as his friends. One way was to go hunting for pop bottles that could be cashed in for real money. He would then beg friends to use his reward on his behalf to buy some treats for him. Second, was to convince an understanding clerk to make exception to his mom's rules. The final and most harsh one was when he had to go get groceries for his mom. Steve would simply go nuts to have a treat but knew the clerk would not allow it. His last resort was to sneak a couple of Tootsie Rolls or Black Jacks and slip them discretely into his pocket while worrying intensely that the county sheriff would be waiting outside to haul him to jail. He says that it did not feel good to do that so he would simply leave the appropriate change on the end of the counter when he left. On a couple of occasions he said his efforts were not very slick and when he was caught, the clerk asked if she should put it on the family charge slip. Living in small communities everyone knew the problem and all did two critical things. First, they prayed for him and second they did what was right. That meant he was reminded constantly that his health was incredibly important. We all need to remember this lesson that when it comes to children, a little care, especially the consistent and loving kind, goes a long way toward making the world a better and healthier place.

Steve's lifelong goal was to stay as healthy as possible. After hearing and hoping that cures lay just around the corner for the first 20 years of his life, he just accepted that he would have this disease for the rest of his life. He always says, "There is a lot more money in treating diabetes than in curing it." He really loves the blessing of good health, and wants others to understand the joy and significance of being healthy. God created us in His image and if we honor that image, we all have a better experience in our worldly lives. The message Steve constantly states is "An ounce of prevention is worth a pound of cure - stay healthy by living healthy. " He has not only learned about the whole health and wellness deal but he has studied, analyzed, tested, recorded, and systematized the process of healthy living. Remove stress – be engaged and challenged – practice creativity - eat properly – exercise regularly - stay positive – take supplements – measure change quantifiably and do it all every day. Since knowing Steve I can count on one hand the times I have seen him take over the counter drugs. He always believes that the best way to treat illness or injury is with natural methods. He sincerely understands and lives by those rules and has since the 1960's. He is always responsible and has been granted unwavering power and intelligence to make it all work by God.

I grew up under the guidance of a mother who was educated as a home economics teacher. She really understood the difference between a house and a home. She taught me by example demonstrating good eating habits. Our meals always consisted of all four-food groups. She always planned timely meals. She also worked hard to keep her cottage as shiny as a pin. She cleaned the cottage, made the beds, washed the dishes, baked pies, cakes, and cookies. Her goal was to teach me all the domestic traits and I learned them well. I had no idea how important these lessons would be for the life that I was destined to live.

Fitness and activity as a kid were both very important in my life just as they were for Steve. My mom and dad both emphasized staying physically fit, and competing in different sports activities occupied a lot of my free time. In living with my husband, I was re-educated about staying healthy and living well. I had married a man who loved sports, exercised daily, and had his own radio and television shows about exercise and nutrition. He trained many of the top athletes in the region and also trained competitive bodybuilders from across three states. A normal routine for me was spending the day with my second grade students at school and spending the evening at one of our health clubs for a full workout session. Cardiovascular exercises, aerobics, and weight training became a passion for me. I became aware of good and bad sugars and all of the ins and outs of the diabetics' life. The completely healthy lifestyle regimen was setting in, making sense, giving me confidence, allowing me to be a fitness model, and it changed my world. I was on billboards, in newspapers and on TV ads. I was meant to inspire others just like Steve. I was learning all of this from someone who is supposed to be sick. Instead I was learning what everyone should know and value. We became a team that lived happy and healthy every day. Not just talking the talk but also walking the walk. We were passionate about and truly believed in the product/service that was both our life and our career – Health and Wellness. We worked really hard to be inspirational, positive role models to everyone we met. Neither of us had any clue just how valuable and necessary our lifestyle would become as we moved from being a couple to being a family.

Chapter Five

*M*y love of children obviously kept me extremely motivated to become a mom. Even though I wanted to get started immediately we waited four years before everything seemed right for us to "go for it." It did not take long before the signs came on. Baby coming? I hope so, but I could not trust an at home pregnancy test. I simply had to go into the clinic, take the pregnancy test and then wait for my doctor to call with the results. This must be a legitimate and formal evaluation. When the nurse called me I was teaching at school and I learned the news right there in the midst of my big family of second grade students. I could not tell anyone before Steve, but it was tough not to just stand right on top of my desk and scream at the top of my lungs "We're pregnant. I am going to be a mommy. This is not just a great day. This is the greatest day of my life."

Steve and I had decided that neither of us would miss any part of our child's life unless it was simply impossible to be there. There was no question in our mind that we would cherish the gracious blessing of parenthood to its fullest. We both also believed that love is felt from the first minute of life and that it lasts forever. Nothing about this family was destined to be taken for granted. That commitment started from our first scheduled visit with my physician and from that moment forward I attended every checkup with my best friend/ husband by my side. In pregnancy two concerns grew at each step. First was the health of our child and the other was my husband's impatience. His attitude is that all people deserve full respect and if you have an appointment with someone you are either early, on time, or you are disrespectful of the person waiting for you. For that reason if our doc was late, even by five minutes, for the scheduled appointment he would go right into the nurses' quarters to remind them we all live by schedules that we must keep in order to pay for such things as medical insurance and physician visits. It embarrassed me, but it did not take long before our appointments were on time – laced with meaningful communication and respectful honesty.

His participation in all elements of our child's health and well-being were also part of God's plan because without his experience, clarity, timeliness, decisiveness, and passion many of the things to come would have been much harder. We shared everything together. There were no secrets, surprises, or unknown feelings. It was several visits into my pregnancy when I finally asked the one important question that was floating around my mind. I did not really want to know the answer but I did need to know. "Is there any chance of having a diabetic child?" I told my doctor that Steve was diabetic, and he was quite surprised by that. He pretty much dismissed the question. He simply told me that if both of us were diabetics it would be a bigger concern. I simply accepted his answer as the truth I wanted to hear and then I moved on with all of my passion, energy, and love into a mode of living so healthy that nothing bad could ever happen to the baby that was growing every day into our first son or daughter.

Does a name make the person or does the person make the name? I/we have not even met him or her and so naming is a really random job of luck and discretion. If our baby asks why he got his name will I have an interesting, inspirational, and believable response? I felt like the miller's daughter in "Rumpelstiltskin" while trying to figure out the perfect name for this soon to be perfect child. As a teacher, the decision was very challenging to me. When I say my associations with past students caused certain names to be more attractive than others I totally mean it! My magical mirror showed me the image that answered the question. The reflection was of a quiet, yet confident boy who marked my heart in a way that I could not forget. His name was Eric and when I told Steve he got a sparkle in his eye and said "Eric the Red." His love for legend and especially Norsk legend weighed heavily on his response. "Eric the Red" was apparently a strong, athletic warrior, adventurer, settler, and leader and my husband quickly agreed that it would be a perfect name for our son.

My heart and soul were both committed to give both my baby and me the most happy experience during birth. One of my big commitments was to be as fit as possible so that both of us would be at our peak of health and prepared to recover from the physical challenge. I was now eating and exercising for two so I trained just like John the Baptist preached. I appreciated the importance of preparation for God's gift of love. Because all great works of God begin with great preparation, I worked to be fully prepared. I lifted weights, conditioned my core, participated in aerobics, and ate primarily natural fruits, grains, and vegetables. I was apparently too good at this and the happy baby inside me went overdue, and more overdue, and even more overdue. Twenty days after we expected the miracle to occur, my "nesting instincts" took over and I worked like Cinderella, scrubbing the floors and organizing the castle so that everything would be as perfect as it could possibly be. This waiting and wondering was certainly part of God's plan because I learned early that all that we are and everything we have is according to His plan, not ours. My theme song became "All Good Gifts" from the Godspell musical.

We thank thee then, O Father, for all things bright and good,
The seedtime and the harvest, our life our health our food,
No gifts have we to offer for all thy love imparts
But that which thou desirest, our humble thankful hearts!

Finally, the blessed day had come and after walking a lot of laps around our block I wished upon a star, and that wish had come true. I started feeling crampy and the intensity was a brand new feeling for me. This must be it! I called Steve home from work and we hustled in. When he took me in to check my progress they smiled and said that we were too early and sent us home to wait a little longer. Again I had to play the waiting game. We went home and the labor began but not with the intensity or frequency to merit our return. I slept another night at home and we went in the next day to be induced. Would it be real this time? Why was God making me wait and think, and ponder so much at what would this project and responsibility of being a mother really be like?

It was a cold December evening as many of the evenings had been. Yet, there was a quiet, peaceful aura to this particular night. The snow was falling softly and the moon glistened above shining a light through the frosty trees. It was a magical night. After more than a day of induced labor our long awaited gift arrived just in time for Christmas. He was beautiful and perfect in every way. He seemed so fragile. When I first held him in my arms, my heart was full! There was a mixture of exhilarating joy, an amazement beyond words, and a glorious gratitude to God. I was holding him, but knew that from this moment on, he would be holding all of my devotion. I am truly blessed! After nearly twenty-four hours of induced labor I had given birth to a special little boy and now life as I know it has changed. As I lay in bed that night, I relish in the fact that my long ago dream has come true. I am a mom! I gaze out the window, and with a sparkle in my eye, I look up to the stars and make a promise to myself. "From this day forward I will become not just Eric's mom, but I will become his "fairy godmother." I will sprinkle magic dust along the winding path of his perfect life for as long as I shall live."

As Hans Christian Anderson once quoted, "Every man's life is a fairy tale written by God's fingers." It became crystal clear that Eric was born to us for a reason. God chose Steve and I to be his parents. We both took that calling very seriously. We felt an overwhelming responsibility on our shoulders. There was a certain sense of mystery involved, but we were ready to take on this challenge and be victorious. He was born just minutes after our community voted and announced that it would build the largest sports dome in the Midwest. His dad believed that was a statement of destiny. We have never expected anything but greatness for our new son and so a proclamation was sent throughout the kingdom to announce the birth of Eric Charles Clute and the first of many celebrations occurred. These celebrations would continue throughout the years and become a common thread in bonding our family together.

I took leave from teaching for over four months and my happiness and purpose seemed complete when I was engaged with motherhood. Jiminy Cricket though, stayed perched atop my shoulder reminding me that the school year still had about a month and a half left. My conscience kept getting the better of me. Despite knowing that it was not what I wanted, I knew that I had to finish my contract. I had a responsibility to my dear students. My job now was to conjure up a solution. I knew I had to believe in the love of the good fairies that were all around. Then, with unexpected joy, a benevolent and magical female appears and offers much needed assistance. My fairy Godmother had appeared and ironically it was my own mother. She volunteered to help and champion the cause for being the perfect caregiver for our son. She loved all of us, and wanted to help bring good fortune to our family. Abracadabra, the dilemma was solved, just like magic.

I returned to work and the time passed by quickly. It was important for me to continue nursing Eric during this time. I truly believed that the nourishment he was getting from me was a powerful, and life enhancing potion that was meant specially for his healthy growth and good keeping. My milk was filled with everything he needed to grow healthy and happy. There is no substitute. I would nurse him before leaving for school and then Steve would bathe him, dress him up, and drop him off at my mom's house. Steve enjoyed their private and special morning time together. This was his son, and there was a lot to teach him. Steve was always busy teaching everything by his actions and he learned to start the day with a smile and always leave with a kiss and hug. After Steve dropped Eric off, my mom would take over until I returned at the eleventh hour, or in other words lunch time. She would use the special powers of wisdom given to her, to magically swirl around her house distracting Eric's tummy rumbles until I breezed in the door. I was quick and organized, as we moms learn to be. In a total of forty minutes I would drive from my school to my mom's splendid house, nurse Eric, eat something myself, and then jump back into my carriage, and vanish into thin air until my final return at dusk.

The lifestyle of a working mom was all okay but it was not the life that I wanted for either my son or myself. I wanted to be mom – not the teacher who tried to be mom when I was not busy with school. The next school year I took a leave of absence. There was no way I could distort the logic that staying at home to raise Eric fulltime would be the best decision for all of us. I knew I couldn't pay someone to love him and watch over him the way I could. I was born and lived waiting to enjoy the blessing of motherhood. Raising children to be normal, average human beings never crossed our minds. His destiny was to be an unusual individual with many strong characteristics. We wished for him to have spectacular qualities and to live each day with a sense of wonder and awe. Our days were busy and filled with activity and adventures planned solely to inspire his creativity and growth both mentally and physically.

His dad inspired him early by placing a basketball hoop in his crib in the hospital nursery. From that day on he just loved playing with any kind of ball from the day he arrived. He enjoyed throwing them, catching them, hitting them, and kicking them. Even before most children could walk he became adept with his skills. He was like an apprentice, wanting to learn about everything. He loved all the sports and all the attention he received when performing. We set up basketball courts, baseball, football, soccer fields, and hockey arenas outside and even inside. The energy and excitement these games brought him was spectacular to observe. He also knew how to be still. Eric loved being read to, and sharing the classic fairy tales with him enabled me to go back in time and revisit my childhood. He would sit for hours building towers, and designing his own sports teams using cards and figurines. He would strategize and memorize basketball and football plays that he believed would work right there on the carpet in our family room all by himself. He would sit and explain them in great detail to his dad when he returned home. I was astonished by all that we learned each day about each other. Legendary deeds were being performed every day and we couldn't wait to share them with daddy.

Eric soon became daddy's "sunshine man". He waited patiently every night for his daddy to return from work. The moment he heard the garage door open he would jump for joy and a spark would light up in his eyes. He would run into his dad's arms and receive a high "whoooshkie" which meant that Eric jumped while daddy lifted him from under his arms and he sprang to the roof as many times as Eric wanted to fly. The magic would start all over again and last throughout each and every evening. He enjoyed mimicking his sports' heroes after watching them on TV and we went to every professional, college, high school, and elementary game we could find. When he got home from spectating it always lead to a new game on our "home court." The next day would start all over again but never exactly the same. Every day was a new and exciting one for all of us. A quote by James M. Barrie became a wish for Eric. "When the first baby laughed for the first time, it's laugh broke into a million pieces, and they all went skipping about. That was the beginning of fairies. And now when every baby is born its first laugh becomes a fairy. So there ought to be one fairy for every boy or girl." Eric's world was fun and joyous and we worked carefully to keep it that way. All seemed to be right with the world.

Eric never had a problem sleeping at naptime or at night. Steve and I both believe that if we stimulate him physically and mentally during the day, then at night he would be exhausted and ready to sleep through the night. I remember there were only a few nights where his behavior became a mystery to us. He would wake up in the middle of the night and start wailing uncontrollably. Rocking him back to sleep just didn't satisfy him. Steve was always intuitive about what he needed when I needed help. In this case he would grab some crackers and juice and bring them to his room. Calmly, Steve would turn on the lights, feed him and there just seemed to be a quiet connection between them. It was kind of instinctual and seemingly unusual. We always just wrote off those episodes as normal behaviors. He just needed a "late night snack." Was this a beguiling sign? Should we have begun a connecting of the dots? Was his metabolism abnormal? Was diabetes in his future?

Chapter Six

Eric was growing up and becoming irresistible to everyone he met. He was no longer a toddler and we knew it was time for a sibling to take up residence in our enchanted kingdom. It is far too easy to treat him excessively and we certainly did not want to wreck him forever. After a little conversation and consideration – including financial and intellectual analysis - the decision was made. We will have our second child. I had an easy pregnancy again. They were all easy, but the deliveries were a different story. Eric took me 24+ hours after inducing labor because I was so late. Now our second little one is on the way with a determined attitude to reach the pot of gold at the end of his rainbow. When I went to the hospital it was all great and I intended to have a completely natural birth. Labor seemed to be going well, and then, just like an evil spell had been cast, my baby's life was put into a tailspin. His heart rate began to decline and we were told he was growing weak. I was told and manipulated to change labor positions to loosen the umbilical cord around his neck. I felt like the room was swirling and I wished and prayed that the doctor had the power to say "abracadabra" so that everything would be all right - just like magic. Unfortunately, the magic did not happen. Everything was in a whirlwind.

Suddenly it became life threatening for both my new son and I. Steve and I resorted to prayer and within minutes a decision was made. An emergency cesarean delivery was initiated. Spontaneously and just like magic, the spell was cast "Izzy Wizzy, let's get busy". His heart was getting weak, then stopped and within seconds I was put under, and the procedure was performed. When I finally woke up I felt like I had been in a trance. I was not able to be present for the birth and I really felt I had missed out. It seemed like moments and now I was suddenly awake and hoping earnestly that I was a new mom with a very important question to be answered. Is the baby okay? Is it a boy or girl? Those questions just started rolling out together. I wasn't there to experience the astonishment of it all. Another miracle had occurred and I wasn't able to experience it. Instead I will relish the description as my story telling husband would tell it. I only fear that it might be a bit of a tall tale like his fishing adventures….and that is good I guess. It does have a very happy ending.

Steve told me that the birth was a miraculous event. Our second birth was not normal by any means - it was unusual. He made a grand arrival. He was a real fighter and seemed determined to become a part of our world. We welcomed him with open arms. Steve even cut the cord and lifted him from my abdomen. He claimed that he smiled as he laid there in my stomach. How many men could or would experience this kind of grace? In some wonderful and yet mystical way I felt like I had actually been present for my son's birth through the presence and clear, specific, emotionally charged, and spiritually inspired description by my husband.

It was springtime with blossoming flowers, birds dancing in the yard, and all living things waking up to grow in the beautiful warm sun. Best of all, in this happy, new day, another beautiful prince has ridden into our kingdom on a wild, bucking horse called "Caesarean". It is again time for a new beginning. When the nurse brought him into my room and placed him in my arms a ray of sunlight reached down and touched my heart. A warm tingle pulsed throughout my body. This brave little man had been given the gift of life for a reason. We survived, he survived an incredible challenge in his first moments. What would ever surprise or scare him? He will be fearless, strong and now the whole, wide world has a brand new sparkle and glitter that starts in his heart and eyes. My happiness seemed complete. Psalm 92:4 expresses that happiness, "For Thou, O LORD, hast made me glad by what Thou hast done, I will sing for joy at the works of Thy hands." We named him Joran, an English derivative of my dad, George's name. It was also the English name of the father of Superman, which of course was appealing to Steve. It is a different name because of the way he came into the world – atypical, different, exciting, and most important successful. Another miracle had occurred, and I expected many more. The lesson I had to learn, was to keep my eyes open, so I would not miss the next one. God works in amazing ways and with God, all things are possible. "Before I formed you in the womb I knew you, and before you were born I consecrated you; I have appointed you a prophet to the nations." Jeremiah 1:5.

Eric and Joran became best buddies. They were inseparable. Just watching the interaction between them was priceless. They were good, kind, sweet and at the same time physical, competitive, humorous, and filled with energy. Many days I felt like Geppetto in the classic fairy tale "Pinocchio". I worked hard to instill the qualities of bravery, truthfulness, and unselfishness. I believed that one day they would become "real boys" filled with love and understanding to make all of the right choices at all of the right times.

We did not have a huge house with private rooms so the boys shared a room and when the day started for one, it also started for the other. They were always and immediately ready for all of the new adventures of the day. As a full time mom, I negotiated schedules to cooperate with the highest priorities of my little team. Usually we would get right into playtime. We tried to get physical to promote growth, healthy circulation, mental stimulation and to give focus to the energy that was exuberant in these morning hours. After strenuous activities we had our mid-morning snack. I was always keen to making certain that my boys would not be wimps so we would always have a physically competitive event wrapped around their mid afternoon snack. I knew that much of a child's learning takes place during the first six years of life. A child learns more, and faster during these years than any other time in life. You do not use formal lessons or teachers because the best learning occurs through play. Parents and childhood care givers need to foster natural learning through play activities. The key is to encourage curiosity, creativity, and learning development by actively interacting and doing that without an adult supervising all the time. Besides being fun and connecting more deeply with you and other children they play with, it will give the essential skills needed to succeed in school and life. Our time between snack time and dinner time was when we had great talks, playful competitions, created things, and sang songs and it always ended with a growing energy and enthusiasm for Daddy's return home for dinner.

Chapter Seven

*O*ur daily routine runs quite smoothly. The joys of motherhood definitely outweigh the sorrows. Life seems to rush by like a speeding train. We are constantly jumping on board so we do not get left behind. Steve and I agreed we wanted to have more children. Before we were married he completely feared the responsibility of fatherhood and now he is completely thrilled by it and the joy that he shares in each waking moment with his children. I especially wanted to find a way to add a little princess to our royal family. We shared the question with Eric and Joran and they thought it would be COOOOOL. After some real planning and assessment of our means and the ways we could manage more children, our decision was made.

In the process of bringing the third sibling into the world I had to accomplish some planning, question answering, and marketing to both my husband and the soon to be siblings. Where would he/she sleep? How would we afford food, clothes, toys, and a bigger car? These were questions, and I resolved that with a little of my own magic fairy dust I would answer all of them including the need to convince Steve that we need a new and bigger house. Plus we really should get moved in before the baby comes. I have a couple of months. Fast means less pain and suffering doesn't it? Our little cottage beneath the tall trees is a beautiful built but small house. It sits amongst great neighbors and friends, but we need more space. I am now focused on finding a different, larger, more perfect house for our growing family. I am the shopper because it was always in my fairytale to have a big house, a big yard, and a big family. The fairy tale remains the focus. Steve is conservative and not much into fairy tales (other than mine) and he tried very hard to convince me that we could add on or wait until the right time to buy the right house. Yet, after drawing up unacceptable remodeling plans and shopping, negotiating, and complaining he came reluctantly to the same place as me and we elected to sell our home and purchase another.

He did the math. He did the budget. He told me the price and now it is up to me. I found our new but a little outdated and I easily see room for change. There was lots of space to play and grow both inside and out. We were on a golf course which made our backyard even bigger, more impressive, and more fun. I did remodeling to the kitchen, bedrooms, and converted the office into a dining room and it was good. I worked hard to keep the house as shiny as a pin, just like Snow White. In the future I would grow to learn that houses and yards are not the value of families but instead a home is anywhere that love, trust, loyalty, fun, and family are constantly present. Sometimes the value of simplicity is hard to really understand.

In our world, we never had a problem conceiving when the decision was made. As I began to grow the boys asked questions. What will he/she do when we are playing? How much will the noise bother regular life? Is it going to be a brother or a sister? What will its name be? Can it go to games with us? How long will it be before it can play games with us? Catch balls? Kick balls? Wrestle? Play defense? We got all of these answered even down to the names. Once again it did not take long and before we knew it we had our third little prince, Gregory. We announced to the world his name would be Lee Christian in honor of my mom's dad and Steve's great grandfather. It was the day of the ND State Powerlifting Meet at our gym and Steve posted his name and size on the 30 X 40 lighted sign on the street for all of the world to see. We were proud and excited by our third boy. Everyone agreed that it was a great name but back at the hospital and away from all of the excitement my mom objected. How does this work? Isn't it honorable to name your child after your grandfather? Grandma did not like the name or the idea and so without counseling from the home team I decided she was right.

When the boys and dad came back bearing gifts for me and the new baby I told them we needed to change his name. Despite Steve's disappointment, Lee Christian became Gregory Lee and now that name fits him perfectly. Most importantly, my closest friend in the whole wide world – my mom - was happy. I am amazed at the power a mother has over her child even though the child is all grown up. I learned an important lesson that day and I hope it stays with me as my children grow. I learned that even the most simple things can be made hard if we do not listen and accept our children's actions and decisions with an open mind and an open heart. If we have done our job well as parents then those actions and decisions are the result of the foundation that we have built within them.

We marvelled at the instant bond that developed between the three brothers. I was fascinated by Gregory's calm and cool disposition along with his dazzling easy smile. It was a match that only could've been made in heaven. He was immediately, and is even now at nineteen years of age, the greatest joy to everyone he meets. He has an easy smile, sense of humor, and sparkling eyes that denote an ambitious and testing approach to life. His fantasy and now his ability to tell an incredible story make him the life of our party and probably many others. I truly believe his presence is a gift from God to help us relax and take our mind off all the rigmaroles of life. He is a constant reminder from God, that through his blessings, we can always live with faith, knowing the joys always outweigh the sorrows. It is crystal clear to me that our life is fabulous. We have handsome, intelligent, and exceptionally athletic boys who love to sing, read, make friends, and play constantly. Most importantly, they love being together. They love being with us. Every day is a fairy tale. But as in all fairy tales there are mysteries as to what was to come for all of us.

Chapter Eight

oran is two now, and possesses several of the "Seven Dwarfs" qualities. He was sometimes "sneezy" or "dopey," but he was mostly "happy." Eric is four, and has new qualities that we had never noticed nor did we have reason to be suspicious of. He was sometimes "grumpy", "bashful", or "sleepy". These qualities were out of character for him because he had always been such a happy, bright, and busy little guy. He rarely stood still and always had a lot to say. His behavior presented itself time and time again and questions started to come to my mind. Steve recognized classic signs of juvenile diabetes. Extreme thirst - he would ask for juicy juice pouches many times during the day. Of course they elevated his blood sugars and dehydrated him further. Frequent urination - he went to the bathroom many, many times and would wake up to go several times at night which further messed up how he felt as his body became more and more dehydrated and starved for carbohydrates. Drowsiness - he sat on the couch and watched favorite videos over and over again in the middle of the day. With no insulin his brain had no fuel to light up the neurons that are needed by all of us to think and move normally. Usually at this time of the day he would want to go outside and play. His muscles though, were wiped out because they could not process the sugars and convert them to the energy needed to move about normally.

His attitude and life pattern had really changed. I wanted to believe that he was growing up and these were just normal traits of children. So what if he was thirsty, and went to the bathroom a lot? So what if he liked watching TV? He cannot always be happy. Sometimes he has the right to get angry just like anyone else. He was a child. I knew all about children and there are always surprises in how they behave. It is no big deal. My stomach started to churn. Why was my husband so concerned? I just wanted to escape from all the thoughts that were running through my mind. Could this all be real? We just had our third baby and I am crazy busy caring for him. If we were going to have a sick child why did God just give us a new baby so fast and easy. This will not make it better it will make it more costly both in time and money. This cannot be real, not now. Then I stopped and refused to let my brain go to a dark place. We agreed that he needed to be checked out. I set up an appointment for the next day. I promised myself that I wouldn't jump to any conclusions before we had some solid facts.

The next morning we all went as planned into the clinic. They took his blood sugar and some other tests. A quick check-up was performed. Then we met in a conference room with the doctor and a special diabetes nurse. I felt there might be some disappointing news, but I refused to accept it. I felt a shot of nervous adrenaline. The heart wrenching diagnosis was announced suddenly, bluntly, and with the full fear and reality that this was not the happy ending to my fairy tale. In the blink of an eye my son, our baby, the cutest little kid in the world – in my heart and mind - had become a type 1 Diabetic. He had a DISEASE! Could this be for real? Are bad dreams ever this real? How could our perfect, little angel have this disease? What did we do wrong? I nursed him almost two years. That should have been the way to keep him healthy and to make him grow healthy. All of these sordid questions kept running through my brain. How had I sinned to deserve this? I couldn't believe it! A sick feeling started in my throat and fell to my stomach like I swallowed an ice cube. A wicked spell had been cast and there was no way to stop it. Or was there? Can he outgrow it? Could it be temporary? Can we feed him something different? In make believe, I could say "One, two, three!" and the magic wand could swing through the air and "poof" the spell could be broken. There was no magic wand anywhere to be found. A sword had pierced my heart instead and the excruciating pain had only begun. This is not death. This is the greatest living disaster, eternal torture. "My God, my God, why hast thou forsaken me?" Matthew 27:45-46. This was not Christ's suffering but I did ask the same question because I could not deal with or understand the pain in this moment.

Next, we were introduced to the doctor who was selected and trained to help us deal with this life altering news. We did not know him because we had never before had a child with diabetes. He was a stranger but he was the doctor who specialized in juvenile diabetes care and treatment. He began by telling us that he was a dad of sons with this disease. He said he had suffered with bouts of depression dealing with his sons' dilemma. He continued to paint a very vivid and real picture of doom and gloom regarding Eric's diagnosis. Listening to his agony of defeat was neither comforting nor helpful to us at this point. We had just received life changing news for all of us, and the communication we received from the doctor in charge was more disappointing and incredibly discouraging. Was he part of this evil plan? Is this the same diabetes that my prince charming has lived with every day that I have known him and every day that he has brought energy, hope, joy, and love to those around him? Where are the jubilant leaders in the fight against diabetes? They are the people that I need.

The nurse was ordered to give our little four-year-old angel his first insulin injection. She forcibly held his hand while she pricked his finger multiple times trying to get a large enough sample to re-test his glucose level. Once this was determined, an insulin dosage could be administered. The nurse in this moment and action again made me think of a wicked witch who was determined to poke a never healing hole in his body and watch him die just like in Sleeping Beauty. Eric was confused and scared. The shock, our shock, his shock and the soul wrenching news were more than any of us could take. He began crying hysterically. Every professional became more intense and this experience was overwhelming. Knowing diabetes as I do now, I realize that his elevated blood glucose level probably impacted his reaction to the circumstance and so, when activities ignited a fear, that fear was not going away suddenly, especially when people he did not know or understand were pressuring him to rapidly accept multiple pokes, prods, and injections without even asking his thoughts or engaging him in deciding about it. How could that needle fit into his bony fragile little arm? It must be done every day – not just this once. Forever, not just until he grew well. This just seemed unspeakably cruel. The harshness, insensitivity, and cruelty in this procedure was more than I could take. I had to leave.

Steve was as though he was in a different place and he was so calm and in control- it scared me. Just imagine his mind on this day and time. It had to be the saddest news that he could ever hear. I will never know what this did to him. He has lived with this intense challenge and responsibility each day. He must have replayed every disgusting thing about diabetes in his mind immediately when we learned the news. Some people say that just as major accidents happen, your life flashes before your eyes and I am sure that is how this news affected Steve. Now I must forever fear that if anything ever happens to Steve due to diabetes, the trauma and/or loss would impact Eric even more than before. Everything Steve does or lives through from this day forward will be a precognition of what might be to come for his son. Instead of withering in fear and disappointment Steve stepped confidently and comfortably to his "sunshine man" and took all things into his control.

He wrapped his arms around Eric and it was as though the Holy Spirit had entered the room with him. Steve has a powerful spiritual existence that suddenly presented itself in this place of fear and trauma. He told the caregivers that we could let him calm down and that he would take care of the injection later in peace and privacy. But that was not acceptable. They said it would be harder if we waited – ha!

It was never a problem again but waiting was apparently not in the book. Since Steve had no other options, he took the needle from the nurse and began to speak with love and comfort to his shocked and afraid little boy. Steve spoke of God, basketball, and sunshine, and Joran, and his mommy, and his bike. Daddy told him that he loved him and that Jesus would never allow him to be hurt or sad because of diabetes. He told him that he was glad that now they were more alike than ever before. He administered Eric's first official insulin injection and then it was over. It was just like magic, as the trust and love between them became evident. It was once again unusual. Daddy was there but there was something extra within him, alongside him, or all around him that just made everything and everyone around him feel and act differently. "And after you have suffered a little while, the God of all grace, who has called you to his eternal glory in Christ, will himself restore, confirm, strengthen, and establish you."1 Peter 5:10. Daddy has suffered "a little while" "with this" and now he assumed a presence strengthened by God that was unusual but beautiful and he made it all better. As I sat in the waiting room, the shrill screams subsided. I began to cry bitterly. He was so young, and so innocent and so good, kind, and sweet. Why couldn't this happen to me instead? I felt helpless. I wanted to make it all better for my little sweetheart. My sense of sadness was overwhelming.

I began to pray. I am a new mom and nursing my baby. I have millions of things to do and care about every day. How can this be real? I know that I cannot do this alone and so I asked God to give me the extra strength I knew I would need to handle this diagnosis. I thanked him for the blessing of my best friend, my dear husband. At the same time, I needed the wisdom to understand why we were given this challenge. I needed His guidance and continued support in being the best mom I could be. And finally, just like every other prayer I've said since I was little, I asked for continued good health and happiness for all of us. AMEN! I had grown up believing the Lord gives us what we need, but we have to do our part. Why wasn't God doing His part? How could God let this happen? Apparently, a bargain was being struck. A lesson was to be learned. My son had this disease, but I believe God spoke right then and there to me and said. "I will give you what you need to deal with this disease as a family. You need to have a continued belief in Me." God's grace is good and so I shall be too. We will overcome and grow better from this challenge.

Right then and there my faithfulness and motherly instincts kicked in and a renewed strength surfaced. All of the doom and gloom will end. No more! I have not felt compassion, personal kindness, understanding or real life, trauma management intelligence from the medical community today. The diagnosis we have been given is for real, forever. I knew no one could or even should sugar coat the disease and all of its life threatening complications. But how you learn of it, approach it, spontaneously live with the disease, and accept it as a forever reality is a monumental undertaking. For those who know little, it could be viewed as a death sentence or on the other hand it can become a reason to live each day to the fullest and then after having lived well with diabetes you have done something unusual. How many people really do appreciate life every day and live it to its fullest. None of us know when our last day will be. Perhaps this would be a lifetime reminder and inspiration for me to live each day a bit more fully and overcome each and every challenge we face together with the same kind of love that I witnessed in my husband as he overcame fear and suffering in the clinic - that is what I need. Love, faith, and a storybook diabetes hero who is the love of my life will be my weapons against all the odds of diabetes complications.

Eric's hero always has been and is his daddy. He watched his daddy brush his hair and teeth every day and he also saw him take his shots day, after day, after day. These two activities were seen by Eric every morning for more than four years. He knew the routine and it was easy. No complaints, no pain, no suffering and all positive and fun from Dad. Perhaps Steve was always conscious that this could someday happen. Eric understood what his daddy was doing because it was explained to him in a way that was not scary that made sense. He saw a happy, joyful, strong, athletic, caring, Godly, and fearless man live each day with the disease that they now shared. He believed his daddy could do anything …and he could. Steve made Eric feel special and important every moment of our little boy's life. He taught Eric far before this day that he could be anything he wanted to be and he reminded him on this day that nothing had changed. "Yes, Eric, you have diabetes, but so do I." Sure, it broke our hearts to hear the reality of the diagnosis, but we knew we could handle the "curve" in the road together as a family. Our son has a disease that, if controlled and monitored, was not terminal. Our job now was to emphasize and make Eric believe his life was significant enough. His life had a purpose. Teaching all of us that the bad things we cannot change, we simply overcome without bitterness. We can't change reality, but we can change the way we view it. Our challenge has been issued. Now it is time to win the battle.

Chapter Nine

Caring for three young sons was a new way of life for me. I was adjusting to the demands of motherhood as well as getting familiar with my new role as a mom of a son with diabetes. Joran was an energetic toddler who chased after his four-year-old big brother constantly. Greg was just a baby and so he was brought along to everything and watched from his seat as we entertained and taught him by our actions, and attitudes. We lived each day to the fullest but with a clear and conscious new understanding. We focused on our new family rule: "Diabetes is not going to take charge of our world. We will take charge of the disease that has now moved into our house. We will continue to live our dream, our way. "The feelings, experiences, emotions, and passion shared will be etched in my heart forever.

Eric went through the "Honeymoon Phase" for the first few months after his diagnosis with ease. This gave me some "false" hope there had been a mistake and a misdiagnosis. I went through a brief period of denial. He still looked the same and enjoyed all the same things as before. His blood sugar levels stayed good in the normal target zone (70-120 mg/dl). Steve had to bring me back down from my cloud and explain this phenomenon as common. Eric was still making some of his own insulin during these early months. He was still a type 1 diabetic, and would be for the rest of his life. This would take a while for me to process. How could our life take on a fairy tale ending now, after the news we have received. I went through "mother panic." Could we all still live happily ever after? What if my beautiful little boy takes ill and dies? What then?

C.S Lewis once said "someday you will be old enough to start reading fairy tales again." This was the time for me to reacquaint myself with the magic that was so powerful in all those stories I grew up with. Every story always has a good guy who is kind and innocent just like Eric. This character usually is subjected to some kind of misfortune, like Eric's diagnosis of diabetes. There will be some bad guys. Throw in a difficult situation, an eventual solution, a whole bunch of magic, and most certainly a happy ending and you've got it! Suddenly it came to me. Why not? What's really changed? I can still live the fantasy - the dream - the life that I want and need. I can take my family on a little trip away from the "facts." G.K Chesterton said, and I quote, "Fairy Tales are more than true; not because they tell us that dragons exist, but because they tell us that dragons can be beaten." These were words of wisdom for me, and from that moment on, I was determined to slay those dragons. This game has no rules, only requirements. There is no clock that says this one is over. The game with our dragon is every minute of every day with every intellectual, physical, and financial asset on the table. Losing in this challenge is not an option.

We pledged to live as normally and happily and healthfully as any family. In my heart, I sent out a decree that would be proclaimed throughout the entire kingdom. It was a promise made that even though we wanted Eric's life to be no different than anyone else's, we really didn't want him to be normal either. Our wish for him was to live an unusual kind of life with joy, adventure, dreams, and a whole bunch of magic. We wanted to be the kind of parents who lead our son and his brothers to exceed their own expectations and to climb every mountain with energy, enthusiasm, and a plan to win.

Our life now became disciplined with certain responsibilities and processes that we all must achieve. The first essential step in the morning that had to happen before breakfast was to check Eric's blood sugar. Joran sat next to Eric the same as Eric had watched his dad. Joran was always extremely inquisitive and always thoughtful. He watched closely and became a part of the daily ritual. We would say the familiar nursery rhyme "this little piggy went to market" as we chose the finger.   I tried to make it a quick, one prick try. His soft, but bony little fingers rested so gently in my grip and as his trusting eyes looked into mine I knew he was counting on me to finish quickly and painlessly. We would play a little game and see who could guess the number that became visible within about 20 seconds on his "tester". He liked to play and it distracted him for a while. Actually, these little games were therapeutic for me also. The little games gave me minutes away from the constant guilt, disappointment, fear, and frustration of watching him deal with what every day seemed to be a really bad deal for all of us.

Depending on the magic number for the day that flashed up on his glucometer, I planned his breakfast. Normally, he ate a simple breakfast including a bowl of cereal and some juice. I purchased the cereals without processed sugar. Joran and Eric's favorites were Rice Krispy's, Kix, or Cheerios. They became Steve and my favorites also. If his blood sugar was high, then we would wait to have a low carb breakfast of protein, like eggs and higher fat meat like bacon along with sugar free juice later in the morning.

Every meal required evaluation prior to preparation. I always checked his glucose again before lunch. Our diet was then planned to fit his status…the "reading". As with most households my little guy, Joran, would go down for an afternoon nap and Eric would either nap or play quietly by himself so that I had some time to rest and recover myself. After lunch was the perfect time to give Eric freedom because after lunch I never had to fear his blood sugar dropping and becoming a problem.

Glucose tablets were always close and handy in our house, car, yard, and world. During our busy and active schedule, either at home or away, a low blood sugar problem could be fixed immediately by feeding Eric a couple of the "big, expensive sweet tarts." As our day finished up, a last glucose check was performed before bed. Testing was and is a constant activity in the diabetes world. If you think having juvenile diabetes just means you live a normal life and take a couple of shots each day you are really incredibly wrong. The challenges of this disease, like most others, are constant, demanding, and continually life threatening.

In the early months after Eric's diagnosis, we administered his insulin injection before bed. Loading the syringe with exactly the precise amount of insulin was a monumentally important procedure. I felt an incredible amount of pressure to get it right. What if my eyes didn't count to the exact correct line that is marked in such tiny print on the syringe? What if I accidently gave him too much or not enough? Would I destroy him and his life by my own very miniscule failing? I had to trust myself over and over in knowing that I just wouldn't screw up. I could not second-guess myself all of the time. As I administered the actual shots I would often feel like a devious wicked witch from those classic fairy tales. His little arm was so tiny, skinny, and his skin so soft and tender. I felt like it was demonic that it was I who had to load up the syringe and day after day stick that sharp and sometimes painful needle smack into the little boy, whose every pain I would gladly assume. I hated needles and getting shots myself. Now I had to give one to my precious little angel. There was something so cruel about all this. How could God just sit up in heaven and let this happen? The All-knowing and Powerful God of all things had to know what we were both going through. It truly broke my heart every time.

The Bible says it best in many ways but in Romans 8:17, I read "We must also share in his suffering, if we are to share in his glory." I snapped myself back to reality and suddenly became the good fairy who always successfully and joyfully fulfilled the task at hand. The syringe was filled with a life-saving potion for my precious son. God understood our shared suffering. Eric's beautiful blue eyes looked into mine and we seemed to understand each other's pain. In our common pain we also learned to enjoy simple pleasures more easily and greatly. Mommy could always make everything alright. That is a gift none of us mom's should ever forget. When you are tired and stressed and all out of energy for your babies just remember they need you to make their things right even if your things are wrong. What a blessing as well as a responsibility that one should never neglect after having assumed the role of "Mommy!" To make Eric's life right, I needed to finish the injection jobs quickly and then hug him passionately and tell him "I love you." This became a ritual. This was a constant and unfailing fact of our daily routine. These acts constantly reminded me Eric's life was my life and he depended on me and trusted me just as much as I loved him. I knew this shot had to be administered, and then our lives could get back to happily ever after.

The diabetes educator and doctors all said the evening snack was important and so we always had our bed time snacks and then it was off to bed for both of my boys. (I struggled with trusting that Eric's insulin would not cause him to fall into an insulin reaction and that he would never wake up.) I played it with a full stomach at bedtime because I thought it was better safe than sorry. My faith was steady in the belief that extra carbs before bed would surely take him through the entire night. If he woke up with an elevated blood sugar reading I would be content because that was better than worrying all night that he would drop low when I was sleeping.

At times I would feel overwhelmed with the constant responsibility of caring for a diabetic child. When these feelings hung heavily in my soul, I thought of Steve in order to overcome. Steve had learned to live successfully as a self-sufficient type 1 diabetic at a young age under his mother's supervision. He has lived unbelievably well and healthy for 52 years with the disease. This is despite the fact that at the age of three his physician told his mom to expect him to enjoy 15 or 20 normal years of life. I think ever since that time he has been entirely committed and programmed to make people wrong when they underestimate him.

His mom and dad let Steve freely run the Dakota prairies with his friends for hours every day without worrying about him. He played on the baseball diamond all day with his friends without a care for blood sugars or insulin reactions. He hiked and biked, built forts, and wandered through sloughs and tree stands alone or in the company of other little boys. Who watched over him to make sure no harm would come? They bought him a gun when he was seven and let him go hunting by himself or with his friends and they did not teach him to fear the surprises of diabetes. More simply he was just made aware of what they were and how to deal with them. He bought his first mini bike when he was only nine-years-old and rode freely on the highways, gravel roads, and prairie trails without a glucometer or snacks to recover from a low blood sugar. He was taught to live freely and without fear and instead he learned to always be aware and in control of how he felt both physically and mentally. He grew to be uncommonly confident, resilient, and powerful. Steve was given control. His parents cared with all of their hearts, but they taught him in a way that just gave up his existence and safety to the power of God.

We too work to empower Eric and as we have hoped, prayed, and planned, he is growing into a great, big brother. Every day he becomes more aware of the world around him. He is learning to be so responsible, so loving, and so forgiving of everyone and everything. Even at this young age he is recognizing the signs and symptoms he felt from inside his body. He knows when he feels sluggish, and has low energy his blood sugar level is high. That means he needs to do some sort of physical activity and drink a large glass of water. He understands the water moves the food through his system quicker, and therefore, he feels better soon. He also knows when he gets hungry, ornery, or confused, like his brain isn't working, he needs to get some sugar quick. He knows well enough and is confident enough to tell someone reliable he needs help. He is growing up and growing wiser every day.

Joran and Gregory grew into reliable and loyal brothers Eric could trust and love. Perhaps it was because of the easy, casual love and trust that Eric freely shared with them that they gave it so thoroughly back. The bond that developed was unusual. Joran grew to be intuitive to Eric's needs. I remember Gregory rarely needed or wanted to be away from things or go down for his nap. His jolly disposition and love of cuddling and coddling by all of us gave relief to the constant care given to Eric. Eric and Joran always watched out for each other and genuinely cared about each other. Their independent worlds also seemed to revolve around Greg's dependence on them and me. These qualities are learned in families who love and respect each other. Children need to know at a young age they are loved and feel it every day from each other. Jesus said it best in John 13:34, "A new command I give you: Love one another. As I have loved you, so you must love one another." Caring for a person with a chronic disease of any kind must be handled with patience, kindness, and a sensitive heart. All children should learn these qualities from those whose examples they see. I would tell you that there is a great benefit in clearly exemplifying this as a parent - the sooner the better.

With Steve's loving example acting constantly to inspire me, I became the mother who began the process of teaching my sons how to believe in themselves. While I taught Eric to live with this disease each day, and to prove it cannot limit either his wellbeing or his ability to succeed I was also teaching his brothers the same lessons. Steve's input, experience, attitude, and expertise concerning diabetes were always very good, introspective, and helpful. It is always reassuring to know that we are working together as a team – it is even better to know that my teammate is a proven winner.

I was "doubly blessed" with another mentor who combined with Steve for more than 100 years success in managing diabetes, and his mom, Delores, was my other teammate. I could always find testimony and insight when dealing with the everyday challenges and experiences. I had to admit I needed help and then I learned to give up my pride and accept the help with a grateful heart (Seems this is a beneficial lesson for all of us when it is learned.) Perhaps I needed this in order to achieve God's plan for me. I have learned this gracious respect for help is a necessity if you want to remain physically, mentally, and spiritually happy, healthy, and wise while continuing to grow through any challenge.

As the years went by, the reality of parenting was constant - Eric and Joran grew and changed. Only Eric's diabetes seemed to stay the same. I kept thinking that somehow it will go away. He will grow out of it. I would wake up from the nasty dream that I was sleeping through. Instead, the conclusion became clearer every day that DIABETES IS AN ENDLESS, GREEDY DISEASE. There is an endless medical to do list: test blood, give shots, eat perfectly, exercise enough, be alert to signs of high or low blood glucose, nutrition label reading, teach friends' moms and teachers what diabetes means, purchase blood glucose testing strips, prescription refills, higher priced health insurance, more regular doctor appointments, insulin supplies, skin creams, low carb foods etc. These were all part of a necessary routine, but only part of the whole picture. I was learning that family support, daily care, correct treatment, unconditional love, and a strong faith that all that we are and will become is part of God's plan were all pieces of the puzzle I was building in order to control the effects of the disease and give Eric a healthy, active, and enjoyable life.

Maintain the balance - insulin, food, and exercise. Keep that blood sugar constant. Food raises blood sugar levels while insulin and exercise lowers them. Seems pretty easy and basic but every day is different and each one brings constant and diverse new challenges.

As North Dakotans, we enjoy four seasons. Fall brings the end of warm weather and mosquitoes and leads to the beginning of school, Halloween, football season, and lots of falling leaves. The boys love it all! Sports and activity are central to our diabetes management. Activity leads to eating more normal food and keeping Eric's cardiovascular system in top condition. Eric's blood sugar and happiness stay constant as a result of our outside activities. We walk around the block searching out and collecting beautiful colored leaves. We shoot baskets at the tons of hoops as we walk around our one-mile circle. We plan and run football plays to use in the constant games in our front yard.

Freezing white weather of winter brings the sleds out of storage and we seek out the biggest and best hills in the Red River Valley and adjacent Minnesota lakes country. Games move inside. Our kitchen, dining room, and living room are a running track and ocean. A favorite game unique to our family has me on the couch equipped with pillows. The boys dodge from behind one chair to the next attempting to reach safety at the far end of our 22-foot long family room while I improve my throwing skills pummeling them with pillows. Suddenly the same area magically changes to an ocean with pillows on the floor representing boats. They jump from one boat to another trying to be successful. If they didn't jump and land on the boat they would sink into the deep brown ocean to be lost forever. Another fun indoor game was our incredible scavenger hunts. My clues would lead them from one mental or physical challenge to the next until they reached their final destination and the amazing but imaginary prize we had selected before the game started.

I remember birthday parties in the beginning of December. We would have a large group of kids downstairs in our basement playing basketball, dancing to "The Chipmunks," laughing and wrestling to the very end and being declared the winners with a loud "pin" from the referee. Once Eric was wrestling with a buddy to the bitter end and instead of hearing "pin" we all heard an ouch and scream. Eric had mistakenly left a needle in his pocket and it had stuck into his buddy. This would be painful to anyone but what became more painful was the thought of Eric's used needle from his blood poking someone else. AIDS is a major issue and now a new problem had surfaced. We had to immediately take action. The young boy's parents, who were good friends of ours, needed to be notified. They were cool about it but concerned, and we all agreed that a blood test at the clinic should be taken. Everything turned out fine but this innocent accident could have been a big problem with severe health issue. Once again the reality of the disease hit home and the severity of its impact could be life threatening.

My husband and I both are huge sports fans and participants. Steve has been a volunteer coach for more than 1500 games (multiply by 2 or 3 to know how many practices he has led) in all sports through the years. It would be easy to lose track of just how many, and we have attended thousands of professional, college, high school, elementary school, and other traveling games in our married life. We obviously agreed that sports, would be an important feature of life in our house and undoubtedly it has been. Sports have been our entertainment, social activity, fun, and relaxation. We probably could have retired now on the amount of money we have invested in tickets with our family of seven. We also pledged that their studies, music, the arts, diverse interpersonal relationships, and a balanced life of unusual experiences would be integrated into our tight knit circle of love. We wanted to give them the tools to be active, and to become independent, gifted, and successful contributors to their churches, families, communities, and the world. Steve always wanted to minimize dependence on insulin as much as possible. He believed less chemicals equal a longer and better life.

We refused to buy any digital Xboxes, computers or other things that would make our kids sit and idly waste their time. The first electronic game came as a gift from Uncle Mike. Despite our fears it worked out fine because they all loved active entertainment so much that the electronic games were only a last resort when not enough energy remained to continue moving around. They only played very occasionally and had to buy their own games with their own money which made it even less of an attraction. Steve intentionally stressed a love for sports in order to help lower Eric's dependence on chemicals. Basketball is a first joy for us because it is easy to teach, rehearse, and play both alone and with others. The love of sports probably results from Steve's parents coaching baseball and basketball and all of the joy that my parents found in competition and attending sporting events.

Nighttime was Eric's worst time for elevated blood sugars and because we worried about giving shots at night resulting in insulin reactions that might kill him. When the weather was decent enough, and even when it was not, Steve would take Eric out and overcome the reluctance and boredom of walking and running for no good reason by giving him a basketball and then challenging him to do new and unique ball handling drills at the same time. They would do them together. They would go out at nine or ten and dribble for between one half mile to a mile even in below freezing temps. Needless to say his insulin needs disappeared rapidly. Another basketball game Eric loved, especially when his blood sugar was high, was a really hard physical challenge that he thoroughly enjoyed. I would count and he would quickly run down the stairs, pick up a basketball, and shoot a basket in our basement basketball court and then run back upstairs, take a breath, and then repeat again. Sometimes he would even dribble the ball up and down the steps. He kept track of his baskets or I kept track of time and we always totaled the baskets at the end. Results were recorded and the goal was always to better the score from before. Eric was having a blast, felt great, and his blood sugar level was dropping back into the target range. We always conjured up fun ways to stay healthy rather than ways to treat illness.

Spring led us back outside in the warm and wonderful weather. Bikes were brought down from the high hooks in the garage, and we would ride laps around the two mile and half mile circles where we lived. Baseball and soccer became the new pastime. Robins' nests were spotted in the trees and bunnies were chased down unsuccessfully. Soon sprinklers came out, along with the water slides, pool and golf clubs. Dad's mowed and chalked baseball diamond, high jump pit, and the all mighty trampoline also adorned the "Clute Fields." No season passed without a focus on fitness.

Children love fitness and learn fitness in simple and subtle ways – if we create that experience for them. Think about that when you put them in front of a television, electronic game, or computer and leave them to grow up there with a machine teaching them right and wrong, happiness and sadness and at the same time that you do not have to speak with others to have fun and really live an exciting life. As a parent with that strategy you will lose in the game of raising great kids who will love you.

During all of the seasons our highlight and favorite place to visit was The All American Athletic Club. It was our home away from home. It was daddy's gym. We loved it for many reasons. The boys could run, shoot baskets, play in the tunnel maze, swim in the pool, bring their friends to the special camps, visit with all kinds of every day adult athletes, be praised for their unbelievable skills, and just be free to move and create new dreams. This was great for me as well because I enjoyed my time with adult visits, workouts, whirlpools, lot of stress relief and relaxation, as well as some time alone. I was fulfilled every time because it was so good for all of us. If you are ever at a loss for a quality and regular family get away just go and find a home away from home in your local gym, fitness center, or community center. The value you get from being physically active is returned not only in multiple ways but also for multiple generations.

Chapter Ten

re-school is a huge milestone in the life of both a mother and her children. It is the beginning of measurement of your preparing that beautiful little extension of your heart and soul to be a human being by themselves and on their own. We chose a private, Lutheran school because it was small and also taught the values we felt were so critical in this changing and challenging world. For Eric and me it was an especially big change and event. I was giving him up and trusting the teachers that he would be guided and watched over by to keep him safe from harm. He attended Tuesday and Thursday afternoons. It was critical to both his physical and mental performance that I made sure he had a good lunch. I took his blood sugar reading before he left to help organize his afternoon away from me at school. I informed the teacher that he was a child with diabetes. She pleasantly informed me that she had a child with diabetes a previous year and knew about the disease already.

I still felt the need to review basic information about the connection between the disease and my son. I reviewed the low blood sugar signs to look for. She reassured me snack time took place in the middle of the school session. Leaving him there was a first step toward independence for him and me. He needed to be in charge of his life now and the disease was a real part for him to manage now. Each day it got easier to leave him. I enjoyed the one on one with Joran and Greg. Eric's needs were being met at school, and the constant responsibility I felt, was removed for a few hours and placed on someone else's shoulders. Pre-school turned out to be a happy, healthy environment. His teacher provided a supportive environment away from home. It was a positive beginning to his future education and personal development.

At the start of every school year we repeated the same protocol. We introduced Eric, along with all of his gifts, to the teacher. All of us were very careful not to dwell on the fact that Eric was a child with diabetes. Some teachers had family or friends that had the disease. Some were familiar, ready, and willing to learn more, whereas others were ignorant and didn't seem to care much about any of it. As a family, we always knew this disease was a serious matter, but never did it take precedence over Eric's regular school day experience. The teachers were always made aware. Some chose to share it with his classmates for an extra learning opportunity about the disease. Never was it our intention to let this disease label him or make him any more special than any other student. We also did not want anyone to hold this against him. We never wanted him to feel different in any way. We just wanted him to be an equal and all he ever asked for or wanted was an equal chance.

Ironically, we continued working to keep him away from believing he was "average." It was always our focus to teach all of our children to believe they are exceptional and unusual – in many good ways. This helps them to recognize they are needed in the world and that their presence is valuable. I constantly worked to reinforce the understanding that being "unusual" meant you are unique in this world. "Dream Big or Stay Home!" could be our slogan. The pride and confidence he gained from this understanding will stay in his heart forever. As Jiminy Cricket taught Pinocchio in the classic fairy tale, "If you wish upon a star, and try very hard, your dreams really, truly will come true."

As Eric got older he became involved in organized sports. Now I feel an urge to quote a famous link "like father like son." The moment Eric was born his dad placed a basketball hoop in the crib at the hospital nursery. Steve put a Gold's Gym t-shirt over his already closely wrapped body. Steve believed winners never quit and that was what he wanted to teach – "never to quit." Eric loved to make baskets on a full size hoop when he was only two-years-old, hitting pitched baseballs when he could barely walk, and dribbling like Curly Neal….he did it because it made his dad smile. He naturally loved and was encouraged to love physical activity and found competition brought him a lot of joy. Eric always liked to "win." He played hard and was determined to win at anything he played. His dad would never make it easy though and today all of the boys love to beat their dad at anything they can. Anytime Steve loses he tells them it is because he had to bring his game down to their level for so many years it will take a while for him to get back to normal (I would always sit back and watch this interaction with amusement.) Oh, this competition never ends – and it is good.

Indent: This was a time to compete but it was also a time or perfect opportunity to teach about good vs. bad sportsmanship. Eric was a quiet, kind, sweet boy and had many, many, friends. Yet, he had an exceptionally driven killer instinct and losing wasn't an option in his naïve world. He always competed at higher levels that also helped keep anyone from making fun of him or leaving him out of things because of his disease. In his first basketball camp he competed at the seventh grade level – successfully – as a third grader. I admit there was some pressure. Still, it was frustrating to me there were times when Eric behaved poorly after a loss. He would sometimes cry and get very upset. As a new sports mom I was sensitive to this behavior. You really become aware of how your child reacts to losing and winning when you are surrounded by parents of other winners and losers.

Impression is everything in my world – it is what I grew up concerned about. I had learned to be sensitive to the judgments made by other parents. We had numerous talks about sportsmanship and what behavior I expected from him. During these athletic activities he expended a lot of energy. We knew that we had to plan properly before the games. Our constant goal was to keep his glucose level in the target range during the game. We always tried to get it to the higher end of normal right before games. I knew it could drop down by the end of game. Many times it did. Yet, there were other times it would go up. Now the question becomes why isn't this easier? When it dropped, the low blood sugar could cause irritability, anger, and disgust. On the other hand if it went high it also was disappointing and frustrating for him. This imperfection in the mind of a boy who knew what he could do when he felt normal was a big problem.

Frustration with his personal performance would sometimes set in for Eric. He knew when his performance was altered due to fluctuations in his blood sugar readings and that really ate away at him. First, he expected to make it possible for his teams to win. Second, Eric disappointed his team and himself when he could not get this unwanted challenge under his control and away from the things he loved. Ability to perform is never sacred in the world of a diabetic because there are so many unmanageable dynamics that impact everything. Tests, performances, athletic events, even driving to and from school can suddenly become extremely challenging and dangerous due to some abnormality of stress, temperature, a meal, too much insulin, or too little sleep. Who can manage all of this as an adult? Imagine the challenge as a 9-year-old-child.

Eric normally had a very levelheaded and calm temperament. He has a serious, focused, quiet, disciplined, and consistent character. You might call him laid back. Every day of his life had to be spent analyzing things most of us never think about. My eyes were opened widely when I saw how quickly his personality could change based upon his blood glucose levels. A low sugar level causes all kinds of challenges. I had a feeling this was only the beginning of a long road for me to become a happy, supportive, and comfortable sports mom. I had to learn to ignore judgment, or my concern about the judgment of other parents, coaches, teammates, and fans. I was frustrated by the ignorance I had always lived with and now ignorance in others simply made me sad and angry.

My thoughts were that "They are all ignorant. Did they know when their kids were eating a McDonald's drive through breakfast on the way to a game that we had to count calories, inject the proper insulin, get enough rest and time it all out so Eric would be able to perform like they normally did?" We loved the Kingdom filled with care, concern, love, and understanding we had created and we were proud he was thriving as a result of it. I lived to watch him grow to become so good at things that someday the world around us would want to know more about how it happened and then bring some of our magic into their world! Oh my, I was trying so hard to make and present everything so perfectly. Why do we moms worry so much about what other people think about us or our kids?

Chapter Eleven

When people found out Steve and Eric were diabetics they were often curious to know more. They wondered what kind of diabetes they had. I always made it a point to share what I knew. I would tell them that they were both type 1 diabetics, also known as juvenile onset diabetics. They both were diagnosed before the age of twenty, and the antibodies they were born with attacked and destroyed the cells that naturally produce insulin. Only about 10% of all people with diabetes are juvenile onset. It is an unusual condition. I tried to keep it simple, even though there really was nothing simple about any of it. I remember after Eric was diagnosed a mom friend of mine was curious (and worried?) about Eric and how he was feeling. She assumed I had given him too much sugar when he was little. I really had no response to that uninformed statement. I knew it was ignorant but a little bit of guilt set in and stayed a while. As juvenile diabetics they were not responsible for having their disease. They simply had to live with it every day no matter how good they behaved or what they did. It does not go away. I did nothing wrong. This is reality. Every day of their lives when they were out of my presence all I could do was pray that God's plan was for them to be safe and healthy for many, many years. Never again would I pass judgment on any child or adult for their behavior or performance.

They are both insulin dependent, which means they needed to replace their insulin every day with injections. People would ask if the injections hurt. I really didn't know. I just know I do not like shots of any kind at any time. They poked needles into themselves maybe 6-10 times a day. Even though they never complained, I had to assume it did. I could never answer the question of how much discomfort they dealt with every day. I would try to get them to rotate the injection site and to poke different fingers every day to help minimize that discomfort but also to keep them from having big, areas of scar tissue I knew could happen. That's about all I could do. Our family learned a lot about shots and when we complained about any blood tests or injections we were made to feel guilty about our wimpiness. We all learned there was no sympathy given when shots were administered to any of the rest of us. We all learned to suck it up and deal with it. Steve and Eric were the tough ones in our family. We only wished we could be as tough as both of them someday.

I know I should be sensitive in discussing this next issue. If someone mentions they are type 2 diabetics and working on managing it, I will support them, but not without extra words of wisdom. They have a chance to get better and reverse their symptoms. Why wouldn't they want to do all they could? You do not need to deal with all of the headaches daily. It is just not right. Eric and Steve would give anything to reverse their diagnosis. An "abracadabra" comes to mind. Why wouldn't someone take advantage of the magic spell if they could? Wouldn't you go for a 30-minute walk daily and cut down on lousy snacks or drinks in order to reduce the cost of your and our healthcare by 60% and at the same time live a normal, long, and healthy life. It just seems so simple and unfair. (Lord, why not just make a type 1 diabetic healthy every time a type 2 is diagnosed and decides to simply take pills and shots rather than change their lifestyle?)

Speaking of questions, concerns, lack of fairness and understanding, a big question for me is always the same. "What does it feel like to have an insulin reaction or even a low blood sugar?" I wished for a genie to switch bodies – well kind of. I would certainly swap my life for my son's but I would not want to join their club. Because I was caring for Eric and Steve during these episodes, it was always a wonder to know what they were really feeling. It is just human nature to want to know things. Yet, I knew and prayed this wish would not be coming true. I always have felt kind of out of the loop for not knowing. I imagine my closest experience is when I haven't eaten, or have skipped a meal and then go for a long and hard exercise session. I get an excruciating headache, slight dizziness, and a hollow ache in my stomach. I guess I will never know for sure. In retrospect, Eric and Steve will never know what it feels like to not have those feelings. They also do not know the feeling of giving birth to a baby but still, the pain of giving birth stops after a few minutes or hours.

I give up and give in because it is and will always be just the way God intended it to be. Eric and Steve have this disease, but it doesn't rule their world – THEY DO. They need to rule over the diabetes. They are strong, handsome, disciplined, motivated, optimistic, energetic, passionate, forgiving, loyal, and most importantly greatly faithful and faith- driven people as a result of living with this disease. That is an unusual blessing. Diabetes is indeed a challenging part of all our lives, but at the same time we are all discovering our lives are becoming richer and more blessed because this disease is a part of it.

There is a great blessing but the curse is always the fact that raising any child is an occupation of self-sacrifice and doesn't leave much time for selfish pleasures. Sometimes it seemed like I was always tending to others. What about me? Who was tending to me and my needs? As soon as my self-pity buzzer went off, I knew it was time for a night out or a getaway. Maybe a date with Steve, lunch with a good friend, or a shopping spree with my mom would do the trick. Any of those ideas would spark me up and bring me back to reality. Having an outing would refresh me and set me back on course. Babysitters were always easy for us to find. Steve had lots of college-age girls and guys at his health clubs who knew and liked our boys and us. He chose his staff largely by their loyalty, friendliness, happiness, and values. All that worked in our childcares had CPR and childcare training as requirements for the job. We felt good asking them because of their age, energy, reliability, training, and responsibility. They also knew how to have fun and that is what our boys were used to. They were like good fairies to all of us. The benefit for them was that we had cool kids, fun things, a nice house and yard, and Steve knew what their time was worth. He always paid them way more than they made at any job because he said, "What matters more in my world - my gym or my children?" Steve lives by the rules of practicality and real values in everything he does. I was always grateful for those who took up my responsibilities for a while.

Just like our babysitters were very important to us, in some cases they produced fun for our neighbors. The people who work at health clubs are usually fit, personable, and fun. On one spring night I invited a very sweet and beautiful girl that worked at our health club childcare during the days and as a Hooters girl at night to baby sit the boys. When she arrived in her red, Chevy Camaro convertible our next-door neighbor who was visiting in our front yard as we waited began to believe that good fairies visited our house too. The boys said that he spent most of the evening visiting with our baby sitter as they played out in the yard. He also told us that he wished he would have had baby sitters like that one. We should have let him share the cost of her services. It is just fun to hear your friends and neighbors appreciate novelty in even the simple things in life.

Moms should always remember to enjoy the big and small events in life. Whether it is the time away, big celebrations, or even the time alone in quiet corners you must find times to celebrate and be good to yourself. You deserve it and need it. We all do. Even dads need a break! Here is a mother's prayer that I regularly take comfort in.

"A mother's gift is to give life. But in the daily demands of feeding and forming, cleaning and conditioning, tending and teaching, her gift can get lost in the layers. She needs to remember that her work begins with herself. To be attentive to others, she must listen to her own heart. To care for others, she must take time for herself. To teach others, she must act lovingly towards her own body and her time. If she finds her own sparks, she will fan them to those around her. If she frees her own spirit, she will help others soar. If she focuses each moment by being wholly present, she will point the way to holiness and to God. And if she truly lives, she will give real life to the world, not only in her children's bodies, but in their souls."

Passionist Publications

Before Eric was diagnosed with diabetes, Steve and I could take vacations, even though they were short, and they were fun, and relaxing for both of us. My mom and dad willingly volunteered to keep the boys at their house. They loved spending time together. They lived in the same town and spent a lot of time with our family. The boys were so comfortable with them it was very easy on all of us. Steve's mom wasn't as comfortable keeping the boys for an extended amount of time. She was older and in some ways wiser. She was the mother of a diabetic and knew the ropes and she understood the responsibility and didn't want her age to prohibit her from the energy and attention she knew the disease required. These welcome getaways for Steve and I allowed the recovery and refreshing time we needed together and alone. All couples need this time because we are forced by our culture to constantly work and worry about things. Taxes, utilities, jobs, family members, houses, cars, classes, neighbors, disasters, practices, etc. all distract us from two really important things in our worlds. First, our faith, and second our family. Husbands and wives are the basis for much of both of these things and we need to dedicate energy to growth in our relationships. Keep perspective and make the commitment to preserve this sacred relationship with as much commitment and discipline as is required.

Chapter Twelve

*T*here is no way that the team of Steve and Ann would be able to successfully manage our little family in such a unique way by chance. Thank God and give Him the glory! As a teacher and health and fitness leader our Father has prepared us to work cooperatively and effectively to live the lifestyle we really needed to live every day. Caring for a child with diabetes and the responsibility, patience, and love it requires was in God's plan all along. Again, I am forced to realize when we recognize all things are part of His plan the stress leaves and is replaced with His support and constant love.

"For WE are GOD'S WORKMANSHIP, CREATED In CHRIST JESUS to DO GOOD WORKS, which GOD PREPARED in ADVANCE for US to DO."
(Ephesians 2:10)

Think about that next time you think YOU NEED TO HAVE ALL OF THE ANSWERS OR START TO THINK THAT YOU MAKE ALL OF THE PLANS. Just stop, pray, and ask for the answers you need to be delivered to you in His time and in His way. Then just do the best you can, be kind, be grateful, give thanks, trust in the Lord, sing praises, grow in your faith, and enjoy the ride. God absolutely and constantly directs us. Our lives are not left to chance in any way, shape, or form. We do not live according to uncontrolled physical laws like an automaton. Instead, God "works all things according to the counsel of His will" Ephesians 1:11.

After busy days, all of us are usually ready for rest. As exhaustion comes, our nightly bedtime rituals begin. To be good to yourself and your kids, moms have to relax when this time of day comes. I noticed when things were not on schedule and I got frustrated and anxious it simply made everything worse. The struggles were greater, someone could not sleep, and the morning would come with some sort of unexpected trauma. I learned to simplify things, lean on consistency no matter what the time, and make the end of each day look and feel very comfortable and positive by reacting only to things that the kids needed or wanted to accomplish. I would steal Eric from whatever activity was happening, check his blood sugar, and fix a simple bedtime snack. Ninety-eight percent of the times, the boys would head off to bed on their own with Joran climbing to the top bunk and Eric to the bottom. This was predetermined because it is very hard to treat an insulin reaction in a top bunk. Steve and I gathered with them in their bedroom to finish the day with (our collective) prayers.

I taught them a childhood prayer of mine I still recite each night. Many of you have probably heard it. It starts out like this" Thank you Jesus for this day. You have kept me all the way. Dearest Jesus through the night. Love me, keep me, hold me tight. God Bless Mom and Dad, Grandpa George and Grandma Dorothy, Grandpa Charles and Grandma Delores….Eric and Joran, etc……"closing with, "keep us happy, healthy, and safe." When Steve was small their prayer was "Now I Lay Me Down To Sleep." I didn't like that prayer because the words seemed too harsh. "Now I lay me down to sleep. I pray the Lord my soul to keep. If I should die before I wake, I pray the Lord my soul to take," This was scary to me and something I didn't want to be reminded of every night. When you have a child with diabetes, every night represents a real concern that it could be the last night with our child. Knowing Steve's mom like she is my own, I guess that is probably why she taught that prayer to him. If she experienced insulin reactions like I have, the reality of him being gone in the morning probably hit too close to her practical heart to ignore. For me, the reality could be avoided at the end of the day and I never wanted God to think we are ready to give our beautiful son up to Him at this time. That prayer just strikes too close to my real fears for us to finish our beautiful and joyous days with it.

Rachel Carson once said "If a child is to keep alive his inborn sense of wonder without any gift from the fairies, he needs the companionship of at least one adult who can share it, rediscovering with him the joy, excitement, and mystery of the world we live in." This magical individual for Eric and Joran is their dad. Every night he told a new bedtime story. He told motivational and educational stories at all times. He tells stories like he lives his life. Every day, every event, and every thought was a new adventure. This was probably easy for him, but as a teacher, I know not many people could make up twenty-minute stories on the fly that made sense, were real, taught life and practical lessons and ended with passion, energy, and motivation to succeed. His tales would range from fairy tales, to Bible stories, stories about their grandparents, to stories about the boys' lives as successful sports heroes. He could spontaneously spin yarns ideal for bedtime because he could put the boys in a state of relaxation that is ideal for a nice rest and a positive inspiration that helped to mold healthy and creative development of both their character and their rapidly growing brains. He is an incredibly impressive storyteller. Rules we had tried to explain for days, and that didn't manage to stick, could be laid out in a bedtime tale, in one night, if the message was creatively depersonalized. He found a way to analyze a problem or situation that arose in the life of our child, and then he would spontaneously reflect and imagine a plot for the new story. When he discussed situations, the messages or morals would be shared with much higher intensity, passion, and understanding than the real experience could provide. Today they still ask if some of them are real. What a gift it is to dream out loud in words so believable that they become true. Something very magical occurred every night! What a shame they were all spontaneous and unrecorded. I wish I could share them all.

At other times he would open the floor as they discussed the story topics. He would even knowingly invite the boys to participate in telling pieces of the story with his questions. Some nights they would ask to be told about something that was a special interest to them. With incomparable ease he would process the wishes of his listeners, and like a genie, their wish was his command. In cases where they were given the opportunity to choose the story, their opinion or rationale for hearing it would always be taken into account. He would tell the stories so close to real life and their world that even I thought they were true. He was ever and always helping them with the development of their emotional, spiritual, physical, intellectual, and relationship understanding. They always loved the attention and care given to the stories. They would feel strong and clever when they understood the messages and the relations between the story and their real world. They really understood and finished these daily messages with acceptance and belief in the moral of the story. "These things I have spoken to you while abiding with you. But the Helper, the Holy Spirit, whom the Father will send in My name, HE WILL TEACH YOU ALL THINGS, AND BRING TO YOUR REMEMBRANCE ALL THAT I SAID TO YOU." (John 14:25-26) I think that Steve, whether he admitted it or not, was consciously preparing them to be students of the Bible and teachings of Jesus Christ who taught and constantly spoke parables.

They especially enjoyed hearing the true stories from their dad's childhood. They were not only memories of love and special personal situations but they were also, because of the mechanics of memory, episodes that because of one thing or another represent important elements in the life of him as a child. I even chimed in with stories from my past. Because they were real and directly correlated to the questions, fears, excitement, and energy they lived in that day I know those constant stories told while cuddled together on one or the other's bed had a profound effect on their minds. An added benefit was that the boys really got to feel that comfort of knowing their parents as well as they knew themselves. To this day they talk to us about everything from school papers, to girls, roommates, money, etc. How can anything breach that trust, faith, confidence, and desire to do good when it is deeply imbedded in the basic foundation of their being. Every night they would fall asleep in a positive world mixed with reality and fantasy. As mothers and fathers we should all assume a responsibility to share in this way with our children. It is stated in Proverbs 22:6, "Train up a child in the way he should go: and when he is old, he will not depart from it." Where do we want our children to go and how are we training them in that path? Television, internet searches, Facebook, and text messages do not seem like "the way, the truth, and the life" to me.

Most evenings were peaceful and serene. Steve burned the midnight oil many nights after a busy day at work and a playful and magical time with his boys. Steve always said staying up late permitted him to get his real work done, but I knew his main priority was to check on Eric in the middle of each night. We owned four health clubs, and several nights a week he would go there to do work or workout after everyone else went to bed. He is very opposed to underperforming or not aggressively pursuing greatness. Most of his employees would tell you that Steve taught using the same parables at work as he did with his boys at bedtime. He loved to work out, and after the seventeen-hour day was complete it offered him uninterrupted time to train for and by himself. I often expected to wake up in the morning and learn he had died under a barbell loaded with iron in the middle of the night. When he came home he would relax, read, listen to some music but almost always between the hours of 2:00 and 2:30 am he would go to Eric's bed and do quick blood sugar test, deliver an extra kiss, and a final tap on his tender young chest as it was moving up and down in a normal and comfortable motion. I never imagined that through those years he would actually learn to work and live on approximately five hours of sleep a night. I too, almost always went back to their room for one more kiss, one more peek, and one more reassurance that everything was going to be alright. Maybe every mom does this, but to me it was just necessary. I went to bed thoroughly relaxed, knowing Steve too, would be double-checking him in the middle of each night.

I gave my best effort every day to keep the boys happy and healthy. Now that they were tucked safely in bed, I had hopes sugarplums were dancing in their heads, but there was still an uncommon worry. Many nights while tucked in by myself, I would inhale a large, full, exaggerated breath and then exhale it slowly, almost as a cleansing of my heart from all the stress and worry of the day. It was as though I was taking in the spirit of the Lord. When complete, I would feel refreshed, recharged and ready to rest and then awake to face another day. When I gave up and gave over to God I could truly relax and fall asleep, assured that God was there by my side, by our side, and believing once again everything was right with the world. "Cast all your anxiety on him because he cares for you." 1 Peter 5:7

Occasionally, nighttime turned into a twilight zone. A bad dream all of us so desperately wanted to wake up from. Joran slept above Eric on the bunk beds. Sometime during the night, he was magically transformed into Eric's guardian angel sent from heaven. Psalm 91:11 "For he shall give his angels charge over thee, to keep thee in all thy ways." Joran would suddenly wake from a sound night of sleep because he would often say he felt the bed shake and then he recognized the frightful grunting, teeth gnashing, flailing, and moans coming from his beloved brother. He immediately would jump from his bed and run to our bedroom, right next-door, and just like the town crier proclaim "It's Eric, come quick, he's having an insulin reaction." Now you must remember he was only three years old when this started. I do not know how this happened but we do know he was an angel or he slept surrounded by angels and that was a very good thing to feel confident about.

When these events happened we definitely awakened to a strange and eerie world full of demonic power. My quiet erupted into full-scale panic. No one ever trained me for this. No classes taught this. No church sermon explained the reality of saving your own child's life. We would rush to his room, Steve was always first and I followed completely frightened of what I would see. It became like a ritual in bringing him back to us. It was like an exorcism. It was like reviving a heart attack victim. It was real life and death. It was all so unusual. Nothing in my world ever prepared me for this harsh reality of motherhood. What if he would die? I tried to stay calm, not to frighten him.

Quickly, Steve would get glucose tablets into him and only once did we use an injection. After the convulsions would settle, we patiently began to talk to him, not wanting to let him fall asleep and drift into a permanent state of unconsciousness. Repeatedly, we would tell him we loved him while hoping God's power of love would rule over Satan's attempts to steal our wonderful son from us. It was always good versus evil. It was always a battle to the very end.....without even a second thought of losing. "Praise God From Whom All Blessings Flow." After what seemed like an eternal wait, he would slowly and quietly respond verbally when his blood sugar level returned to normal. When he did come around he was always more interested in going back to sleep than I was.

The moments went something like this. Steve would put his arms around him and hold him while making him accept the glucose tablets. He would demand his attention through repetitive and simple questions. He would repeat over and over, "It is going to be all right son. We love you. God loves you. Please talk to me Eric." I would get the glucometer and check his glucose level so Steve would know how low his reading was and react appropriately. When he was in true convulsions and seizures it became very hard. I always wrestled with whether to call the ambulance or to count on God's ability to guide Steve to correct what was always a mistake. When he would come around, I always tried to get eye contact. I would start by asking him simple questions about himself. Obviously, his blood sugar was still very low. Often his glucometer reading would be in the 20's or lower. We likely always overloaded him with carbs because nothing seemed like enough. Glucose tablets were easy, but sometimes it was hard to get him to chew because he could not. Steve would slowly and gently place them in and they would dissolve. I would say we were normally calm after we were with him and we found strength in our faith and the belief that God's will and love was always present during these insanely, heart wrenching ordeals. We believed and trusted he would be okay but at the same time the reality was his life was in the balance and we could not assume anything until we took control. We adamantly refused to believe his destiny was other than one of a joyous, long and happy life. After 10-15 minutes of Hellish intensity, our little prince would return to us. He never remembered the episodes, thank God, and that was okay by all of us.

When I think of these times and the role Joran played I think of the song "Hero" by David Crosby and Phil Collins and the last verse where it says,

"Well it was one of those great stories
 That you can't put down at night
 The hero knew what he had to do
 And he wasn't afraid to fight
 The villain goes to jail

While the hero goes free
I wish it were that simple
For me
Were that simple for me"

David is also a diabetic and I would guess he never imagined the description being one of a little boy saving his big brother from insulin reactions. Joran was most definitely the hero of our challenging health journeys. Just like any classic fairy tale, he knew there was an important quest to undertake. His big brother needed help. Joran rode in on his white horse aided by God's angels and grace. On a side note, Steve always believed it was angels who shook Joran hard enough to wake him every time this happened. He simply remembered the shaking. He removed himself from a peaceful sleep in his comfortable surroundings and took the enemy on, with a strong determination to overcome and save the hero of his world, his big, loving brother. Without this hero surfacing, we never would know the peril Eric was facing, and Eric could perish. Amazingly, Joran, like the song said, would always go free and never ever made a big deal of any of this. He simply knew and rested comfortably in the fact it was the right thing to do.

Our experiences and the journey we traveled had the same eloquent themes that ran through every classic fairy tale. If you need help, ask for it, and the fairies will come. Good deeds will win out. Love conquers all. The weak become strong. The wicked are punished. There are many good rewards, but not without costs! In the end there is always a balance. These themes were from fairy tales. Weren't fairy tales supposed to be make-believe? Why were they making so much sense in our real world? Maybe it's our job to make people believe. Albert Einstein once said, and I quote, "If you want your child to be intelligent read them fairy tales. If you want them to be more intelligent, read them more fairy tales." What do we really want our children to learn in life? Perhaps by not only reading fairy tales but also living them we build determination, value, passion, quality, discipline, creativity, intelligence and character. That is my goal and there is no doubt in my mind it will lead to a happy ending.

Insulin reactions brought us closer as a family, and closer to God. God had been watching over all of us and his grace keeps Eric with us. Many times after these episodes I would literally break down and sob. Eric's life could have ended. We could have lost him. It seemed so close and so easy. The love he received from all of us was the key. We gave it, he felt it, and we all were stronger in the end. Our faith was being tested. Isn't everything a part of His plan? You who have not been tested cannot know the measure of God's power. Prepare yourself, and never underestimate the power of preparation – worship, study, and prayer - and the strength of a sincere and wholesome belief in God. We know the only real judge in this world is He who watches over all things, at all times and in all places. Steve never went to bed after these events – after everyone was safe he always left to be by himself. Once he told me that while he lived alone at law school once he awoke while standing in his small kitchen drinking orange juice and that he felt the presence of someone walking out the door and leaving him there. When he went back to his bed the blankets were strewn around the room and his actual mattress was soaked in water. He said that he felt that it was an angel who came to save him because the door was bolt locked where the person had walked out. He said that there were other stories like this that I would never understand or believe. I will never know or understand what he had to deal with in his diabetic heart and mind after these episodes.

God could've taken Eric to Heaven to live with him many, many times. God had chosen to leave him in our care here on earth. God gives us all gifts to share with the world. I believe Eric's work is not done yet. Living his life with this disease is in God's plan. God is using all of us to share His good news. On my fridge I keep a couple meaningful sayings. One says, "God doesn't give us more than we can handle." The other says, "The character He finds greatest, He gives the greatest challenges to." I ponder these messages often. They continue to keep me positive and focused on my mission. God had a plan for me and for our family. The journey will not end. I just wonder with excitement and anxiety what challenges and joys are coming next. In a sort of childlike wonder, I live excited, and am inspired by the apprehension of finding out.

Chapter Thirteen

$\mathcal{A}$ fter Eric became a diabetic we felt a need to re-evaluate our trips and getaways. We knew caring for a young child with diabetes is a huge responsibility and didn't wish it on anybody. We did not want anything bad to happen while we were away. We didn't want to take advantage of the wonderful relationship all of us shared. I trusted my parents would be able to handle the responsibility, but felt it was now ours to take ownership of. Many of our friends would take trips during the long winter months, and sometimes I felt jealous we didn't do that anymore. I knew there would be plenty of vacations in the future, but for now, this is where we were supposed to be. Parenting is like a business. When you run your own business you ultimately need to be there in order to be in charge. You can have managers and employees who are important to success, but the brunt of the work falls on your own shoulders. You are ultimately responsible for success or failure regardless of all other factors.

It is important to be ready for that responsibility when you decide to have a family. It is not part time and neither is it temporary. When you treat it as part time or temporary you likely end up in just the same place as the 90% of startups that fail. Plan, prepare (live on your own/have some life experiences), become informed (hang around people with children), speak with people who have been there (had children), pray, test your theories, and then evaluate and ask friends to help you critique your ability to live with the commitments that are required. I did most of these things and am glad because otherwise this might have been too much to handle. It had to happen at the right time in my life, with the right person in my life, and with the right faith in my heart to make it all work. Life is a big job but life with a dependent diabetic child is an unbelievably big job. Our prior private getaways would now become getaways with our family. We learned to refresh and relax in an entirely new and different way. I think it is another blessing because now when we were refreshing ourselves we were also refreshing our whole family. We learned to recharge and refresh as a team. Twenty-seven years later we are still doing it.

Sometimes family and friends asked me if I miss my teaching career? I had been home with the boys for eight years. I still enjoyed volunteering at school when I was needed, but my world was full, and I felt extremely satisfied doing my job – a very important job - at home. I sometimes missed the adult interaction and conversation. I joined playgroups for that. The kids played and the moms could visit. It was a win-win for everybody. I didn't like being labeled as a "stay home mom" or "homemaker". I guess I was a mom at home and I was trying hard to make our house a home but, "The family's activity director" seemed to have a better ring to my ears. It was just more descriptive and made my roles and responsibilities more defined and official. More people seemed to accept this job as a real one at least in my mind. It took me a while and some self-discovery to answer questions like, "What do you do all day, eat bon-bons and watch soap operas?" As I grew more secure with what I believe is my calling from God, whatever people labeled me as was okay by me. I knew, believed, and accepted that my place was right here. This is where I belong. God has told me so time after time as I have asked him in my prayers after insulin reactions, before athletic competitions, in quiet moments when everyone is away and especially when I am in the midst of my fairy tale team.

We knew people from many different kingdoms, and if we were open and thoughtful we could learn life lessons from all of them. Leo Rosten summed it up nicely when he wrote, "You can understand and relate to most people better if you look at them - no matter how old or impressive they may be - as if they are children. Most of us never grow up or mature all that much - we simple grow taller. Oh, to be sure, we laugh less and play less, and wear uncomfortable disguises like adults, but beneath the costume is the child we always are, whose needs are simple, whose daily life is still best described by fairy tales." I am playing my fairy tale out and I am still the child I always was. Yet, I am living a unique chapter in my fairy tale that is right out of "The Three Billy Goats Gruff" story.

Three Billy Goats Gruff

Once upon a time
there were three Billy Goats called Gruff.
In the winter they lived in a barn in the valley.
When spring came they longed to travel
up to the mountains to eat the lush sweet grass.
On their way to the mountains
the three Billy Goats Gruff had to cross a rushing river.
There was only one bridge across it, made of wooden planks.
And underneath the bridge
there lived a terrible, ugly, one-eyed troll.
Nobody was allowed to cross the bridge
without the troll's permission
and nobody ever got permission.
He always ate them up.
The smallest Billy Goat Gruff was first to reach the bridge.
Trippity-trop, trippity-trop
went his little hooves as he trotted
over the wooden planks.

Ting-tang, ting-tang went the little bell round his neck.
"Who's that trotting over my bridge ? "
Growled the troll from under the bridge.
"Billy Goat Gruff," squeaked the smallest goat
in his little voice.
"I'm only going up to the mountain
to eat the sweet spring grass."

"Oh no, you're not!" said the troll.
"I'm going to eat you for breakfast!"
"Oh no, please Mr. Troll, "pleaded the goat.
"I'm only the smallest Billy Goat Gruff.
I'm much too tiny for you to eat,
and I wouldn't taste very good.
Why don't you wait for my brother,
the second Billy Goat Gruff?
He's much bigger than me
and would be much more tasty."
The troll did not want to waste his time on a little goat if
there was a bigger and better one to eat.
"All right, you can cross my bridge," he grunted.
"Go and get fatter on the mountain
and I'll eat you on your way back!"
So the smallest Billy Goat Gruff
skipped across to the other side.
The troll did not have to wait long
for the second Billy Goat Gruff.
Clip-clop, clip-clop went his hooves
as he clattered over the wooden planks.

Ding-dong, ding-dong went the bell around his neck.
"Who's that clattering across my bridge?"
screamed the troll,
suddenly appearing from under the planks.
"Billy Goat Gruff"said the second goat in his middle-sized
voice.
"I'm going up to the mountain
to eat the lovely spring grass."
"Oh no you're not!" said the troll.
"I'm going to eat you for breakfast."
"Oh, no, please," said the second goat.
"I may be bigger than the first Billy Goat Gruff,
but I'm much smaller than my brother,
the third Billy Goat Gruff.

Why don't you wait for him?
He would be much more of a meal than me."
The troll was getting very hungry,
but he did not want to waste his appetite
on a middle-sized goat
if there was an even bigger one to come.
"All right, you can cross my bridge," he rumbled.
"Go and get fatter on the mountain
and I'll eat you on your way back!"
So the middle-sized Billy Goat Gruff scampered across to the
other side.

The troll did not have to wait long
for the third Billy Goat Gruff.
Tromp-tramp, tromp-tramp went his hooves
as he stomped across the wooden planks.
Bong-bang, bong-bang went the big bell round his neck.
"Who's that stomping over my bridge?" roared the troll,
resting his chin on his hands.
"Billy Goat Gruff," said the third goat in a deep voice.
"I'm going up to the mountain
to eat the lush spring grass. "
"Oh no you're not," said the troll
as he clambered up on to the bridge.
"I'm going to eat you for breakfast!"
"That's what you think,"
said the Biggest Billy Goat Gruff.

Then he lowered his horns, galloped along the bridge
and butted the ugly troll.
Up, up, up went the troll into the air...
then down, down, down into the rushing river below.
He disappeared below the swirling waters,
and was gone.
So much for his breakfast,
thought the biggest Billy Goat Gruff.

"Now what about mine!"

And he walked in triumph over the bridge to join his two brothers on the mountain pastures. From then on everyone could cross the bridge whenever they liked.

Thanks to the Three Billy Goats Gruff

By Paul Galdone

I live with that same "terrible, ugly, one-eyed troll" named DIABETES under my motherhood bridge and I cannot knock him off the bridge no matter how hard I try. Instead, I will just keep ramming him day after day, night after night and minute by minute until he is broken and gone. That will be the end of this trying chapter in my fairy tale life.

Steve and I must have a little of "Ma and Pa Kettle" in our royal lineage too. Their comedic lifestyle, easy going demeanor, and desire to use simplicity and common sense as their guide was in a number of ways similar to ours. We constantly had exciting and rousing games in our yard. Windows were broken by balls and rocks shot off from tennis rackets and baseball bats. Our boys giggling wildly in the kitchen only to be caught mooning the golfers on the 7th fairway right outside our back door. Micro motorcycles (tiny crotch rockets) and bikes riding up and down the neighborhood sidewalks kept all of us and our neighbors on our toes. Even the plywood, shingled tree house sitting between our three evergreen trees was a statement of independence and ambition. In the same manner as the Kettle family grew to be fifteen children strong, our blessed kingdom continued to grow larger as we announced the coming arrival of our fourth little prince.

In the birthing room before his arrival, I was asked to balance on a large exercise ball to help begin the contractions and speed up the delivery. Perhaps you know the exercise – or at least you may have heard of it. It was a hot summer afternoon, as most of 1996 had been, and my baby seemed anxious to get out of his hot, sultry home. He and I had both been very comfortable living as one for the last nine months. But right there in those last moments before we met I remember hearing the word balance time after time, after time….and it forced me to ask the question, "How was I going to successfully balance all the demands of motherhood with four children, plus a son and husband who are diabetic?" I knew Eric still needed my utmost attention with all the demands of his diabetes. Joran was six and Gregory was only four. What were we doing? What was I doing? Another child? More chaos? Then I knew the answer – "No, it just means more love! That is what I want. I want to give more love to another child who forever will spread the same genuine love that grows from our family across the whole world."

How about this? I really, really want a daughter in my kingdom. That internal drive to have a child of my own gender who will share all of my great love and knowledge of motherhood with is strong within me. Yet, I was so busy and engaged with mothering, I did not really stop and consider one important question. How do I maintain balance? Without much time to contemplate the important question, along with some others that suddenly became apparent to me, another son who is named Chad Michael was born. Steve and I both knew Chads and they were all cool guys. It seemed to be a simple yet strong name. Steve's brother was Michael and a special friend in our world. Chad Michael had a nice ring to it and it became the perfect name for our new little prince. He is another blessing from God. I thank God every day for the blessing he is. His three older brothers had been great advocates of more kids. They were very helpful throughout my pregnancy. And now they were very excited to meet their new little brother. They even made a pit stop at an eclectic gift shop that served their favorite ice cream shakes to get gifts to shower him with. They dreamed and already spoke of the day to come, when his little legs weren't so wobbly and his eyes weren't so sleepy and he could catch footballs, baseballs, hide in the backyard, and play in 2-on-2 basketball games in our basement and on our concrete driveway. After they left me for the night they and their dad even went to the local baseball field to watch the local pro baseball FM Redhawks team as a celebration of their little brother's birth. I guess my teaching him to make monster cookies will have to wait.

We all adored him and his actions seem to indicate he certainly knew it. Suddenly, I knew the answers to my previous questions were right. We would all help raise this new little prince. We are a family and there is lots of love to go around. Perhaps we should have named him "BALANCE" because all of the focus I was demanded to give before was now being given by my three young princes to Chad and at the same time they grew to share more love for one another. He did bring balance into our world. God truly had it planned. Give Him the glory. Now my role is to become the coach, delegate jobs to my team, and inspire them to be the best they can be. They were young, but old enough to want to help. This was something I would learn to do, and I would be confident about doing it. Steve was good with promoting this new way of life. He has always been a great coach with everything he tackles and he was trying to teach me to approach it the same way. This new lifestyle, living as a team and playing the game of life with all their help was incredibly fulfilling and appreciated, especially by me.

This was our fourth child. This was our fourth baptism. I am a faithful Christian. I am a believer and I constantly try to live that way. We always work very hard to choose very special people as Godparents of our children. As we searched for the right person everything seemed so different for Chad than for the other boys. We knew there was a special need and a special role for a true baptism sponsor – GODPARENT. The Book of Common Prayer says

....

Each candidate for Holy Baptism is to be sponsored by one or more baptized persons. Sponsors of adults and older children present their candidates and thereby signify their endorsement of the candidates and their intention to support them by prayer and example in their Christian life. Sponsors of infants, commonly called godparents, present their candidates, make promises in their own names, and also take vows on behalf of their candidates. It is fitting that parents be included among the godparents of their own children. Parents and godparents are to be instructed in the meaning of Baptism, in their duties to help the new Christians grow in the knowledge and love of God, and in their responsibilities as members of his Church.

....

Sponsors should be:

Christian - Only Christians can, in good conscience before God and Church, make the baptismal renunciations and promises on behalf of the candidate.

Regular participants with a Christian congregation for his or her own spiritual growth.

Willing to enter into a long-term relationship with the person to be baptized.

A family member, relative, or friend.

....

The church requires there be at least one sponsor. There should be at least one woman and one man, other than the parents. This provides several persons for the baptismal connection between candidate and sponsors, and creates balance and variety.

....

On Chad's baptism day, he would have been incredibly honored (if he only understood) to know that his three older brothers had asked to be his Godfathers. All that he needed to know about God and love could be learned from them even better than from someone who would only see him sometimes and irregularly. They stood together at the front of the church and together they read their pledge to their little brother. They made a promise to teach him about God and all of his blessings, and to watch over him for the rest of his life. That heartfelt proclamation was absorbed, like a sponge absorbs Holy Water, in all of the members of my kingdom. It had become a cherished labor of love for and loyalty to each other, and the legacy of it would live on forever. That love and loyalty will be a constant stability and security for all of them, as they continue to journey through life and all the ups and downs it entails. The love and pride we felt at that moment was priceless. Why would I continue to worry about the disease that had the power to shake our world? Why worry about who would get it next? I have witnessed a miraculous declaration of love. It is another sign from God. Everything is perfect. I just need to keep the faith and continue knowing and believing. It is all good, if it is all God.

Chapter Fourteen

After the birth of Chad we all tried to settle in to a brand new routine. Eric was now eight, Joran was six, and Gregory was four. They all attended school at a private Lutheran school. We both felt that having them all there had many educational benefits. The Christian themed emphasis that was a part of the entire curriculum scored big points with us. I had devoted my time and energy each day to our family, by spending countless hours creating challenging activities to stimulate their brains and bodies mentally, physically, and spiritually. Obviously, we both believed that philosophy should continue. Personally, I liked the idea of all three brothers being at the same school. They could see and watch over each other every day at school. The smaller class sizes made for more attention from the teacher and the students. And what I felt the best about was Eric would be watched closer and his diabetes would be monitored more personally than in our much larger public school. I just felt better each school day, when I was home and away from Eric that long that he was in good hands. I soon became more comfortable with this arrangement. There would be new caregivers and mentors in his world. That was good and healthy for both of us. I just had to learn to "let go of the kite a bit, and let him fly." I dreamed one day he would not just fly, but soar. Soon he would travel to far away kingdoms and enjoy the journey and all its many adventures along the way just like any other person in the world.

We hoped and prayed a private, Christian, learning environment would be beneficial to our boys, and that it would deliver a positive experience as they traveled their life's journeys in pursuit of their own "happily ever afters." We knew God would guide them every step of the way, but it was important they learn His ways and His words in preparation for the challenges and adversities that happen to all of us. They needed a place where they could learn it, live it, and believe it. They needed to begin setting their own course. I want that mission to be as simple to state as possible – especially as young men. Live in the likeness of God and share the message. I want Jiminy Cricket in all of my boys' ears, all of the time. I want to share the stories, give the examples, encourage the good decisions, and applaud the right things clearly to give them a foundation of strength. When they were faced with dilemmas and decisions that voice that is their conscious should always ask the same question, "What is right? What is wrong? What would make mom and dad proud? What would Jesus Do?"

The years passed quickly and there were always new challenges when raising a house full of boys. I grew up with two younger brothers and definitely knew about this male world. As much as I tried to generate a beautiful, clean, fresh, and wholesome environment, the testosterone just seemed to filter through everything. Because I was the only female member of the household, I was constantly challenged to correct behaviors like burps, farts, genitalia lingo, rough housing, and silly, potty mouth humor. I felt it was my responsibility, as their mother, to filter out the disgusting behavior while still knowing every day "boy" antics would just be a normal part of my life. Teaching them about good manners became one of my many primary objectives. "Please," "thank you," and "excuse me" became staples in their vocabulary. The Golden Rule was a constant lesson. "Do unto others as you would have them do unto you." was constantly intimated or clearly stated. I just had to be reminded they were growing boys and burping in their face could be considered a pretty amusing event. Back to balance.

Steve also lived with a playfulness about him. He enjoyed life to the fullest and wanted to share that enthusiasm with all of us. He was a great big boy at heart. The boys loved to roughhouse, laugh, and joke around on a regular basis. I would sit back and marvel at the closeness all that commotion promoted. Hours and even days would pass and diabetes would leave our world. There would be no reminders evident anywhere that this disease lived in our lives. We were just like other families, maybe even a little more active, enthusiastic, and edgy than some. As I lived it, watched it, experienced it, cared about and learned of it, I BEGAN TO LEARN THAT STEVE AND ERIC HAVE DIABETES, BUT DIABETES DOESN'T HAVE THEM. Perhaps I had known it for a long time because I fell in love with and married Steve, not because he was afflicted with a disease called diabetes but instead because he was so inspirational and motivated in everything he did. His life was inspirational, not only to me but to most who know him and now especially to my sons - our sons. "If it don't kill you, it will make you better" has been his motto for more than three decades.

Our life was good, and our pursuit of happiness, as a family was real. I assume just like any other family, anywhere in the world, we want to be our best and to do our best each day. Steve's positive attitude and healthy lifestyle reassured me that his diabetes was under control. I felt relaxed and worry-free when thinking about him and his diabetes. I truly feel in his master plan he never wants to have diabetes have anything to do with affecting any day or any part of my or our life. It seems as though he has found a deep, hidden power to stay healthy, incredibly enduring, active, and resourceful in any challenge facing us. Is that what diabetes has done to him or for him? Then it is an "Unusual Blessing." He knows my focus needs to be on Eric and the other boys just like his focus was on them and me. He was the sole provider for all our fiscal needs and every day he was a spiritual and physical leader for his sons. He lived to spare me any concern for his health and I cannot even imagine how difficult this would be if he was not physically healthy and mentally happy. He didn't want me to have more than I could handle on my plate each day. I loved him for that, but I knew I had enough care and love in my heart to go around. I felt like God just kept replenishing my heart with love and the tools I needed to grow stronger and more useful to my family and our bigger family including our extended family. As the moments, days, weeks, months, and years passed by, my heart was tested over and over again by fears, failings, faults, and frailties. If only my family knew they all held my heart in the palm of their hands in every minute of every day.

The lifestyle Steve lived, exemplified, and promoted both personally and professionally was working like a fine-toothed comb for all of us. The positive rewards we all received were the blessings of good health and happiness. Steve had successfully lived a full life with the cursed disease that was cast upon him as a three-year-old boy. His body and mind were working like a fine-tuned machine. He had been taking the same insulin for all thirty some years of his life. Then one day he came home very disgusted and confused. He had been in to pick up a bottle of insulin and his pharmacist told him Lilly Corporation was discontinuing that pork insulin product in favor of a synthetic brand. It was like a bad dream. He was floored! What do you mean they are phasing it out? The pharmacist was sympathetic, but it didn't change Steve's life, his world, or the longevity and consistency of his life. He practiced holistic care and consistent, disciplined life practices. He ate consistently. He exercised consistently. He believed his body had fully transitioned over the long, long time of use to become completely efficient at utilization of the pork insulin. He was afraid. He never thought money would cause his consistent source of life to stop producing the lifeline he was connected to. He tried his hardest to get answers from the Lilly Corporation but they simply ignored his requests for a legitimate answer for the change. In its finality we understand profit is more important than people in most major businesses and the change must be managed. Steve tried to find control. He contemplated options with his intelligence and common sense. He tried to come up with an acceptable and comforting plan of action. In the end he couldn't really do anything to change the news.

What was the Lilly Corporation thinking? This is a big deal. People all over the world would be going through some sort of physical change, what is the impact? This is a chemical that he is dependent on just as a drug addict who goes through very noticeable pains when his drug of dependence is taken away. Steve immediately stocked up on as many vials as he could round up. The end was coming though. He expected that he would be going through something unpleasant when his supply was finished. He also believed that over more than three decades his body performed on pork insulin as though everything is normal. Now physical abnormality must occur and be managed.

His last vial was gone and he began using the new Humulin insulin. He felt crappy for a considerable time. Imagine promising to give it and then taking a vital life-sustaining organ away from you. That is how he felt. He seriously assumed a synthetic is a second rate substitution that could be produced at pennies of the cost compared to a real good and naturally created insulin. He kept believing someday soon he would feel back to normal, but really there were no guarantees and he could not know for sure. How many others had lived three and a half decades using pork insulin and were now making the change. He just couldn't trust any of it. He proceeded by being extremely diligent and analytic in trying to adjust to this new treatment requirement for his disease. I would worry and my eagle eyes went into overdrive for the many weeks ahead.

Steve never deviated or complained about this – or really anything – instead he continued with his demanding, normal schedule at work and with his zealous family schedule at home. I would regularly be inquisitive as to how he was feeling. I didn't want to nag, but I really felt the need to know. Our day would always end with a ritual Steve and I started after we got married. We would fall asleep each night with our feet touching under the covers. Throughout the night, if I woke up, I would swipe his leg with my foot, and that would give me the important information I needed. If it was sweaty or clammy, I knew that his blood sugar was low and he needed attention. I would wake him up and inform him that he needed a snack   Most of the time this was a simple, smooth way to avoid what could be a problem. This became habit, and was my own little, unusual technique to casually monitor his glucose when he was sound asleep. Once this little test of mine was finished, I would be able to relax and fall back to sleep. I have awoken many times over the years to wake him in avoidance of an insulin reaction. Now at night when I go to sleep I can do so with the easy, peaceful feeling that God's presence is constantly there to awake me when my husband is in need.

There were a few midnight incidences that turned out to be pretty rough on, not just me, but all of us. I would wake up and my special trick would let me know that he was not only clammy but the sheets on his side of the bed were drenched in sweat. He would shake (kind of like a twitch). His muscles would be involuntarily moving. His nervous system and brain were shutting down and therefore his life would soon be following. I got really scared and I learned, with experience, it was vital for me to stay calm and in control. In these severe instances he would not cooperate. He would resist me and was stubborn in his reluctance to acknowledge there was a problem and the problem was threatening his life. I learned to block out his opposition to the reality I knew. I was gentle and calm, but in an authoritarian way. I would get something with sugar and then I would practice my negotiation with the most unreasonable foe in America. I had to win because he simply had to eat. Sometimes he would feed himself, and at other times I would have to force him to eat. It was very difficult when he was uncooperative because he is about 6 feet and 250 lbs. of rock hard muscle and I am about 135 pounds. He would lock his lips together and blow out and all the while babbling in gibberish speech. The knowledge that his brain was shutting down allowed me to dismiss this craziness but it was always very difficult to listen to. He was like a stranger, and this behavior was so unlike the man who loves everyone, never says no, and makes complete sense in everything he says. Insulin reactions are very unpleasant and anyone who writes diabetes off as "no big deal" should have to treat a type 1 while they are irrational, convulsing, and in danger of losing their life. This is no joke. I just prayed and believed that soon I would have my sweet Stevie back. I always knew once I helped to get enough sugar in his system, and when his glucose was back in the target range, it was like magic, and suddenly he would come back as his normal, loving, rational, and responsible self. This was my prompt and highly spontaneous plan. An insulin reaction is never treated as dress rehearsals, they are always very real and they are very serious occasions. Thank God that in twenty-seven years of marriage there have only been a handful of them.

Usually these occurrences happened when everyone besides me was sleeping. I usually dealt with the "risky business" alone – well not entirely because I know I had a team of angels coaching Steve and me through this every time. Only on a few occasions has my fear and excitement woken up the rest of our family. I did not want them to be alarmed or afraid and I would not disturb them unless I really needed some help. They would simply freak out seeing their dad in this state. The strong solid rock in our world was suddenly helpless, weak, incapacitated, unreasonable, non-communicative, and in danger. He needed our help. It was frightening for all of us. I would work fast and at the same time try to keep everyone else calm and hopeful. At times my emotions would get in the way and sometimes I wondered how I was able to stay sane during these episodes myself. I would be reminded of the saying, "Patience is the ability to keep your motor idling when you feel like stripping your gears." God and the angels were always there when I needed them most. He calmed my nerves and somehow got us all through these frightful episodes. My faith just continued to grow stronger. The boys learned to believe and our faith really grew to make a lot of sense as we lived with His presence. God watches over all of us, and they really felt and understood God and His angels really come and stay with us at all times and in all places when needed. Would He be with us the next time? Would He stay for the long haul? Somehow, we all desperately needed to know the answers to those all-important questions. Our faith and ability to live with confidence and peace truly reflect John 20:29 "BLESSED are those who have NOT SEEN and yet have believed." We learned to simply know God is present in our every minute of every day.

Insulin reactions were always very hard on me whether they were Steve's or Eric's. When we had successfully made it through, I would pray they never would happen again, ever. I remember feeling that I knew what abused women go through physically and mentally. During these episodes I would become very scared. I wondered if he would ever strike at me, unknowingly harm me or one of the kids. How could this gentle, kind man turn violent through his words and actions. It was like a nightmare I desperately wanted to wake from. This wasn't the man I married. Who was this stranger? It's like a "Dr. Jeckyl, Mr.Hyde" scenario. The body in front of me looked like Steve but it really wasn't him. It is like an alien had possessed his body and mind. The only thing that kept me strong and confident was my belief that my beloved best friend and my knight in shining armor would return. I know the risks and power of this cruel disease. It has a wicked, quiet, cruel way of taking lives and changing people into demons during these unusual moments.

My only options in this constant management process was to constantly be alert, constantly aware of decisions and conditions, and to react rapidly and intelligently or else we would lose our beloved dad, husband, son, and brother forever. This is not a problem, this is life and death. Every minute of every day - there are no second chances. There are no magic spells. It is just God, His angels, and I and losing the battle is not an option.

I should clarify that Steve often worked out very late at night because we owned and he managed our health clubs. In order to stay fit and strong he would often wait until the facility closed in order to work out without interruption. This, of course, could cause rapid changes in his blood glucose levels, especially when he was in the midst of stressful events, long days and did not want to take in unnecessary calories before he went to sleep. One night Steve's blood sugar dropped extremely low and my strength was overpowered by weakness and doubt. God tested me beyond my strength. I knew God was with us but I just couldn't feel Him there on this particular night. I struggled to gain control but became overwhelmed and needed something/someone real and present at that moment in time to get me through. I felt alone and needed help. Would they-could they-get here fast enough? I called 911 and within 10 minutes help arrived. These were professionals who were trained to assist a diabetic going through a diabetic reaction, right? Everything had happened so fast. They administered a glucagon shot and within seconds his condition improved.

When he was alert and aware, which did not take long, he questioned why I had made all of the fuss. As a matter of fact he knew the EMT's from our gym and laughed when he asked what the heck they were doing in his bedroom. I admitted I panicked but suddenly I felt guilty. Why did I call them? Why all the commotion? But then again, he could never know how I was feeling. He was out of sorts and couldn't help himself. He wasn't really even there. I did what I felt was best at that fateful time. I left guilt behind and would never worry about that again. I love him as much as myself and when I get scared and need help my reaction is always going to be the right one. I made a wise decision, not a dumb one. Yea, Ann! Someone please give me a high five. I had to trust my judgment and believe I made the right choices. I hadn't been a wimp. God had been with me and assisted me in my decisions. He always was there. My doubt was not with Him but instead it was within me. I would not allow doubt to enter my heart ever again and I thank God for the blessing of phones, friends, good caregivers and a strong heart.

On this one occasion when I needed help it amazed me when my neighbors suddenly were asking what all the excitement was about last night. We had an ambulance, fire truck, and policemen with bright lights and sirens and lots of bells and whistles at our home. I explained what happened as simply and unalarmingly as possible, but knew in the back of my mind they would never really get it. Even my mom called and asked why the ambulance had been to our house. She saw it in the newspaper. Yeah, they could say they understood the medical condition and why the ambulance was there. However, they would never know all of the different emotions and challenges I had gone through and would continue going through on this journey. To the neighbors, Steve was back to "normal". He was once again out playing in the yard with the kids, and visiting with anyone who passed by, but our world was anything but "normal." Would the fiasco happen again? I made a wish I wouldn't have to experience what I did last night again, but somehow I knew that I most likely would. This disease had a power beyond my control. The only person who would be able to tackle this head on was God. His power was stronger than any disease and so I am leaving the matter in His hands. I placed my faith and trust in God's hands and then I never felt alone again.

On a different note there is another point of view I can only guess at. What must a person with diabetes do every day as they see that pump, insert that needle, and inject the insulin that is so essential? They are asked to keep their blood sugar controlled, which means "keep it low." This means a small miscalculation can alter their life. On the other hand if they let the blood glucose levels run high and stay safe from reactions they can look forward to loss of vision, amputations, failed kidneys, heart disease, etc. My husband is positive, happy, and enthusiastic with everyone every day. He does not talk about reactions. He does not care what people think when he acts a little goofy or when the neighbors ask why the ambulance, firemen, and cops were at our door at 3 am. He just deals with it constantly. My son deals with it constantly. We deal with it constantly. What does it all mean? We leave it up to Jesus and believe He would do this the same way as us. Live, love, and laugh and the world will smile with you.

Chapter Fifteen

e always believed one of our many "jobs" as parents was to expose our kids to a variety of different activities in order to broaden their knowledge, understanding, and experiences. Through the years they became artists, musicians, magicians, athletes, mechanics, carpenters, students, landscapers, coaches, and entrepreneurs. Yet, we did not want them to miss out on one real fact. You do not succeed or fail at everything. We wanted both success and failure to render lessons and to give them what it took to help them grow both as competitors and people. How far do you get in the world of capitalism if you do not learn to compete? When they learned about a new hobby, or interest, we taught them to commit to be good at it and to give it their best effort. After experimenting with each one, it became obvious to us that the extracurricular with the most universal interest to them all was athletics. It became a passion for all of them. I think it was the team, the energy, the competition, and the stories that could be shared, stolen, lived, and relived anywhere and anytime. The favorite sport always corresponded to the season of the year. Our family lived in the yard and the driveway and even today when I see friends from the neighborhood where we lived when they were all children they say we lived with our kids and we always had a game or event going.

Competition and physical activity went beyond the yard and it lived in our hearts. We all wanted to live and act like champions and to understand fully what was required and what the results of winning felt like. Steve would mow baseball fields in our back yard. He shoveled the form of football fields in that same yard. He built goal posts in the yard and put high jump poles there as well. Soccer lines were painted in the front yard and every game was a big deal. We never ended without a winner and a loser. The same occurred in our basement during the long winter months when 8-10 friends would come to play basketball on our bare concrete floor or hit plastic baseballs at each other in that same basement. Golf was fun through the pines as well as between the bathroom and dining room. Life was not only a wonderful adventure it was also an exciting game. The fun was always present in the fact that despite winning or losing we all grew better.

Our oldest child Eric's third grade was a thrilling year. That's the year he started playing "real games" of basketball. We played both the Gus Macker 3 on 3 tourneys and the traveling tourneys. We learned that not many competitions were available for his age group so we played in tournaments that included teams two or three years older. Steve set out to teach all of the kids that hung with our boys how to win and how to feel good about doing their best at winning. At school, competitive games began in 5th grade. As Eric passed from year to year our private school did not have a winning basketball tradition. It seemed no one took winning seriously and the interest was in participation. Steve could not accept that you learned to become a winner by losing. He had grown up loving games because they were competitive. It was his way of proving he was not a weak and fragile diabetic. His mom and dad were both high school coaches and his dad was a college athlete. He was blessed with great coaches who knew the game and instilled their love of the game magically into him. He asked how could a school we paid extra to attend offer this extra-curricular activity and just not care if it was a success or failure. What was Christian about that behavior? We sent our children to a private Lutheran school expecting a high quality, motivating, Christian education in all areas of development. God had given all us special gifts, and we knew the responsibility to use them to the best of our ability with a constantly joyful heart. Steve would not allow us to believe losing was all right. He believes that you learn to be a winner by living like a winner, thinking like a winner, eating like a winner, training like a winner and therefore hating to lose. He also believed that if you said someone or something is good and fun then you should not produce average performance.

The whole lackadaisical attitude about athletics and their competitions was deeply troubling to Steve and me. Steve always believed you can motivate and teach people to win. You can also encourage and teach them to lose. He tried to do everything to prove his loyalty and commitment to his family and his teams by simply giving everything he had to dedicating all of his energy, time, faith, and love to make winning a consistent action. His life and thoughts were always based on the ideal that if you are not succeeding everyone better try harder. Steve decided to start a traveling basketball team. He was on a mission. He invited a group of boys who were Eric's friends primarily at school. Eric liked them and enjoyed his time with them. They were young. They were friends. They trusted each other and naturally recognized who could do what and when. Steve's entire faith in success was built around cumulative positive energy, loyalty, trust, and commitment. We also knew many of the parents, and everyone started on the same page. Steve did not go for the biggest, fastest, most athletic or gifted players. He just wanted nice kids who he could teach to become loyal teammates. His goal was to teach the game of life and basketball using the knowledge he had acquired through his years as a player, teammate, business, and community leader. He would teach respect and loyalty first, then skills and sports intelligence. He understands success and worked from the formula that leads people to become successful. His purpose and hope was that every boy would grow as a person, and learn to love both the game and each other. He had a plan and was very aware the principles you learn from being part of a quality team would not stop at the basketball court. He did not want to waste anyone's time and so every moment he was in practice, games, or visiting casually there was an underlying focus on teaching high quality values and fundamental lessons for life.

Parents all know everyone cannot win all of the time but they should also know doing things well and right with the highest quality systems and values available is an unbeatable value for your young children. As they grow older you cannot control who teaches them or how they are taught– they must deal with the fallibilities based upon the values and knowledge instilled in them while they are very young. I suggest you give them the best you can during their early years.

Our new team was successful and Eric thrived. We loved the families and we all became part of an extended family. We felt secure in knowing Eric's diabetes would not have to be front and center. Dad was the coach and would always be able to anticipate and control conditions to minimize embarrassment. He had a sixth sense for sports and it worked for both the team and for Eric. Steve loved coaching and the fulfillment that came with being with the kids. Our family spent our weekends together and learning more about each other. I felt privileged to be able to share this new chapter in Eric's life and our world. He and his teammates were rapidly spreading their wings and gaining self-confidence. We were letting him fly out of the nest, but I knew we would always be present and prepared to catch him if he fell. This team became well recognized in every direction around and it did not end in one year. The group went undefeated in their school ball also. They rarely went to a tournament without coming back with a championship trophy. Many of these boys continued to play together all the way through high school, state tournaments, and several in college basketball. Many of the parents remain friends more than 20 years later. I learned that being coached by your dad does not make anything easy. Steve did not accept weakness or excuses – especially from his diabetic son. HE HAD LIVED IT AND KNEW THE MINUTE YOU LET YOUR

ILLNESS BE RESPONSIBLE FOR YOUR OUTCOMES, THEN YOUR ILLNESS CONTROLS YOUR LIFE. Steve was making sure Eric would make the decisions in his life and his diabetes would have no role in what those decisions were.

This family's activities director position became a full time job. Eric was now nine years, Joran was seven, Gregory was five, and Chad was one. The testosterone was not just filtering through the air anymore, it was a stagnant aroma. The closets were filled with all kinds of athletic shoes, sports jerseys, jock straps, and seasonal sports memorabilia. The garage was plum full with all kinds of sporting equipment. The cars did not fit in. This kingdom of mine was turning into a kingdom of theirs. I was definitely outnumbered. What had happened to my beautiful and organized little cottage beneath the tall trees? I knew it was time to cast a spell. This spell would set a happy medium in our household. I would agree to respect their "real boy world" if they would respect my "real girl world." I grew up liking things neat and orderly. This was a trait I learned from my mom. My boys and their friends needed to agree and commit to keeping a smile on my face and I would likewise do the same for them. The spell worked. We came to an understanding that our mutual responsibility, love, and respect would guarantee that our kingdom would run happily and smoothly for every one of us.

I probably was too intense and focused on living every day with this disease-diabetes in our home. I sometimes felt very isolated from the real world. What was life like for a "normal" family? What kind of issues did they deal with each day? When hanging out with other parents I was reminded every family had challenging situations such as how to get children to go to sleep, how to get them to eat healthier, how to be nicer to their siblings, how to obey the rules. The list just goes on and on. It is always good to talk to other parents to stay in the loop. I just wonder if those other parents were checking the web for new information on diabetes each day. I wondered how many of them kept one eye open all night waiting for someone to run in to tell them one of their children was dying. I had some self-sympathy and really struggled at times with why did this happen to me. I know that even as far back as The Old Testament in Psalms it was prophesied that Jesus would say the words "My God why have you forsaken me?" It is a common question to all mankind. I just wonder about what blessing I might realize from this unusual circumstance.

Another challenge for me was to become a proficient medical researcher. I really felt like it was a huge responsibility and essential for me to stay informed on any breakthrough in new medicines, tools, or supplements for diabetes. The research is ongoing and I felt compelled to follow all of the news. Sometimes the information would stress me out. I wasn't very tech savvy on the computer and always felt a generation away from totally mastering it. Steve would always tell me not to get hung up because he had heard a cure was coming next year since he was six years old. That is about 52 years of anticipation – WHAT? Unbelievable…. that it has advanced so slowly. My husband has an unreasonable belief there is too much money in diabetes for a real permanent cure to be found – or allowed to be found. In his words "This disease and all of the results of it creates unbelievable wealth and that wealth will force this disease to continue to exist." I hope not.

As a result of our son's need to learn to manage diabetes rather than allowing diabetes to manage our son's life, Steve has dedicated his life to providing an automated system to maximize human performance using digital technologies to deliver fully personalized coaching in real time. This technology project has forced a man who really did not like technology much to become an expert on the computer. His work has forced him to work constantly every day to become proficient in the digital world. He has always been proud to be an independent student of the disease. He takes pride in the story of being invited by one of his medical school friends during his law school career to attend a speech by a national diabetes expert. When the speaker asked if there were any diabetics in the class Steve unconsciously raised his hand and was the only volunteer. He then answered questions about diabetes for ten minutes before being told that he will be a great doctor….once again I must remind you he was a law student. Steve is always a step ahead of any new age innovation in the media. He refuses to have any surprises when it comes to diabetes. Technology was everywhere in our world and the boys were just starting to discover all the new ways to stay connected. This will prove to be very beneficial to all of us in the future.

As I matured in my pursuit of diabetes education I discovered that a valuable and reliable resource was readily available in the American Diabetes Association. Steve and I both got involved with the Diabetes Bike Rides. Steve was always contributing to the nonprofit community. He has always been fully committed to giving back to those who needed help. He was the Bike Ride Chairman for several years and when he thought it was appropriate he asked me to take his position. I found it to be very fulfilling. We both took our turns as Bike Ride Chairman over a number of years – even before Eric was diagnosed with the disease. Donations were collected from interested riders and other sponsors and supporters. The donations would be used for research and help for the diabetes community. What a great way to be able to help the cause that has become such an important part of our lives.

We attended the local diabetes roasts each year. It was always a fancy shindig with a lot of pomp and circumstance. I would get all dressed up, get my hair and nails done, and wait excitedly for the big night. This was an outing that was dear to our hearts. It was an evening to beat all evenings. I thought it would be a way to get and stay connected to others who also had the disease or sincere care about it and shared our goal to find a cure. But then as I grew more active I felt the reality was far different from my desire and purpose.

These evenings started with a social hour of mingling and martiniing. Then everyone would find their table and the show would begin. A master of ceremonies welcomed us all and then the protective armor would have to be put on. Brutal statistics were shared, along with the gruesome complications associated with the disease, followed by what was in my opinion further doom and gloom. Was this supposed to be motivating and fun? Was the event supposed to be what I got all dressed up for? I came for a celebration of successes and victories. I want to see advancement and change. My whole life will be about eliminating the pain and agony of diabetes and cheering the people who overcome it and those who really and truly make differences for now that change the future of diabetes. We simply have to unite to eliminate this cruel disease. I had to quit playing the game because I could not plug my ears at the sound of injustice and pain. I had done this as a child, not wanting to listen to bad words. The oracle of cruel disease would continue for ten or fifteen minutes. I think it was intended to tell people who knew it is a horrible injustice to become a diabetic that the knowledge is confirmed. This was just too hard to sit through. With every sentence, a sword swung back and forth into and out of, and into and out of, back and forth further and further into my heart. I know it is a terrible disease. Heart attacks, amputations, blindness, and kidney disease could be around the corner but I wasn't ready to play peek-a-boo. Something about hearing these statistics from a large man with an even larger voice, in a large atrium filled with so many people, was just too large of a reality bite for me to want to experience and handle every year. I think like most diabetics or family and friends with diabetes I needed to get to an event that told me stories of healing, succeeding against odds, and of people being recognized and rewarded for these accomplishments. The people who have the disease or family members with it do not need to know how bad it is. We do not even need to be reminded because you know what? We feel it, breathe it, taste it, smell it, and think about it every minute of every day! There is no excuse for the lack of action to cure diabetes! It is not impossible – commit to this action like my husband and sons have committed to living like normal people and diabetes will be history.

Ironically, the evening would advance with an invitation to sit back, enjoy the delicious meal, and be ready to be entertained by a local celebrity and others who could make lots of jokes and share laughter concerning funny events and frustrating events to most people....not people with a deep, deep, ceded need to cure this illness and all of the faults that it harbors every minute of every day. How did they expect me to just turn off all of my raw emotion and just move on? I was being asked to relax and forget diabetes in the midst of diabetes – the disease that does not sleep, does not get better, does not stop costing financially, does not make sense to cure. This is entirely about the deep-seeded pain and emotions I-we live and breathe constantly, and they had just drilled what I try to forget every day over and over again back to the top of my brain. How many people at this event actually live in my world? Yeah, there were people there who had had their lives touched by the disease and that was comforting, but more were there as financial supporters, not personal supporters. They got a free meal and a tax deduction. What? Why? I think there should be events for those who have successfully lived this disease to laugh and cheer together and there should be another event where they stand up and say "what if this was your child and you lived constantly with this pain – not for weeks, months, or years but instead for lifetimes". Type 1 juvenile diabetics who live from their preteen years into their 60's, 70's, and 80's are the true heroes in this world of diabetes. We send flowers to most sick people and ask how we can help. With juvenile diabetes, we just tell them to get over it and pretend they are normal.

Why is there still so much research, so much information, so much money, so much time, but still no cure? We tried our best and attended for quite a few years, with me always dreading the opening segment, but later we decided there were other ways to support the ADA and its dedication to find a cure. I could not go forever to see no real advances and it became too much of a painful reminder of the doom and gloom diabetes could bring as we all were traveling down the trail. We have decided it is better for our family to go out together and rejoice the successes and blessings of our lives with diabetes. We can do it because in our family it is not someone's problem it is our family's lifestyle. We enjoy the minutes together for many reasons and pray there will be many, many more even against the odds.

Chapter Sixteen

I was going through my days with my newfound understanding each life must follow its own course. What happens to others with this disease has nothing to do with what will happen to my child. There will always be comparisons, but I wasn't going to get caught up in all the negativity. Learning to shrug some of that off was the beginning of wisdom for me. This was our ship. We do not have captains, we have stewards. Each and every one of us was a steward to each other. With respect, loyalty, and integrity this team can accomplish anything. We cannot do it alone but we can do it together and we are together. In success and failure, in pain and comfort, in riches and hunger we speak with one another and share with each other. This is our theme song:

We are One in The Spirit,
We are One in The Lord.
We are One in The Spirit,
We are One in The Lord.

And we pray that all unity may one day be restored.
And they'll know we are Christians by our love,
By our Love,
Yes they'll know we are Christians by our love.

We will work with each other,
We will work side by side.
We will work with each other,
We will work side by side.
And we'll guard each man's dignity
And save each man's pride.

We will walk with each other,
We will walk hand in hand.

We will walk with each other,
We will walk hand in hand.
And together we'll spread the News
That God is in our land.

I had lived through my "Thirty Something" years and was approaching my forty's. Many of my friends were done having children. When asked about it, they always very matter of factly would answer "I'm done." I was never like that, and always pondered the thought of another baby. Here we had four wonderful healthy sons. I keep forgetting one is sick with a chronic disease. Yet, we handle it successfully and well. We had challenges, but everybody does. We were happy and life was good. Why upset the apple cart? I loved my boys, but what if we/I could now have a princess to complete the kingdom and to share my female dreams and excitements with? Was I too old to have another healthy baby? I really wished that my fairy godmother would appear and answer all those thought provoking questions for me. Didn't she have mystical wisdom? I waited for some of those answers, but she never surfaced, and neither did the answers. I decided to leave it up to God. He would consider all those questions and I knew that His almighty wisdom would let me know, somehow. After all, His wisdom was all knowing and the most powerful of all. He is the guide in all I say, do, and experience. I just need to be patient.

It had been months since I had pondered those thought provoking questions. I had put them on the back burner because things were happening so fast in life. The boys' activities never stop. Steve is making great strides to build a huge new health, wellness, sports and fitness complex with basketball, swimming pools, track, fitness, hospitality, children's fitness, hockey, arcade spaces, medical services, business services, coffee, and restaurant facilities were all nearly in reach. Yet, the thought is pretty consistent, and I wonder if God has an answer to my desire for another baby?

Suddenly I started feeling somewhat sluggish with flu like symptoms. I always had believed when we get temporarily sick it is God's way to slow us down a bit. I must need some rest from all of the ongoing excitement. Then it dawned on me and I wondered if my stomach discomfort along with frequent big girl naps meant something more. Could I be pregnant? I went to get a home test and because I knew that I could be I was not too shocked to learn I most definitely was.

Wow, another child! Could it maybe be a princess this time? We were all excited about the news. Life went on as usual without even skipping a beat. But there was an unusual feeling inside of me. It had only been about six weeks but I was cramping and spotting. I know this isn't normal and I went to the doctor to find out what was wrong. I learned that I/we had miscarried. I had heard of friends who had gone through miscarriages, but I never paid much attention. I did not think it could happen to me. I was not taught to expect the unexpected nor to harbor fear in the midst of happiness. That is not my way and for that reason bad things are big surprises.

I felt the profound loss, but I also believed there was a reason this had happened now. God only knows why. Miscarriages are indeed emotionally charged and I had been insensitive to that emotion in the past, when dealing with friends who had lived through this. Here again is a lesson learned through my miscarriage. God opened up my heart to the pain of others, re-emphasizing to me a good friend listens and supports her friends through all of life's trials. I was sad and it was hard to explain to the rest of the family. I didn't have any real answers to their questions. I tried to convince myself the conditions just weren't right for a baby in our world right now. I tried to move on and get back to my routine. I was still a mom to four wonderful boys and they needed my love and attention. Our world was complete for now . Maybe there will be a next time. Steve always believes the answer is in God's hands and for this reason it has nothing to do with us, but instead it was right for us. I too still believed God has his plan, but knew that everything needed to be right. This unknown little angel was in heaven now – alone? No, I guess not really alone, but in the midst of the purest and most humble, forgiving, and accepting angels in Heaven. Perhaps the unborn babies are the angels who welcome us at its very gates. They are probably the most truly blessed of all creation by their purity and love.

The days flew by, and I got back on focus with my boys and husband. We stayed busy and then one day I felt exhaustion coming on again. What does this mean? Am I sick? Could I be pregnant again? I must say pregnancy is not difficult for me. Even though I am older than most mothers, I am pregnant, but this time I will wait to share the news - just in case something unexpected happens. I believe this is a second chance, but how could I know this is the real deal? I felt great and continued with all of my usual activities. This time I passed through my second month of pregnancy and thought, so far so good. Then, I suddenly spotted like before. How could it be happening again? I went in to the clinic and was told the devastating news there was no heartbeat anymore. Why God? Why did you let me get all excited again and then nothing? What was wrong this time? Wouldn't I be able to have any more children?

It took me longer this time to get over the loss. It feels lonely, and no one in my family knows how I am feeling. At least I do not think so. Now we have two little angels holding hands with God up in heaven. The visual image makes me feel warm, comfortable, peaceful, and happy inside. Somehow the sadness slowly started leaving my heart and was replaced by a happy, hopeful feeling. I do look forward to meeting them both someday, but for now, my place is here on earth, working to bring a little bit of heaven to this world and the lives I touch every day.

While his older brothers were busy at school Chad and I had fun hanging out together. One on one time was always cherished and became an envied time by all. As a little three-year-old guy his life was anything but dull. He was amazing. He could do anything while still in diapers any teenager could do. He played every game well. He could lead kids ten years older in what to do and when. People from across Minnesota and the Dakota's would give my three-year-old boy money at halftimes for swishing three pointers while wearing diapers. We had fun, but when the boys returned from school, the real fun began. Eric is eleven, Joran is nine, and Gregory is seven. His brothers doted on him and were teaching him something new every day. Most of it is good, but on occasion it does get questionable. That's what you get as the youngest of four boys. Chad is a worldly boy who is ready for anything that might get thrown his way. His nose had a tendency to grow rather long at times, but with all of our guidance he too was learning to become a "real boy."

My days were enjoyable, and yet I would occasionally catch myself thinking about our little angels up in heaven and wondering if they were the last children I would conceive. Didn't God have just one more angel in His plans He could loan us for a little while longer than the previous two? I still had hope. Visiting with a friend she shared her special, and yet similar story with me. She had miscarried twice and then the next time she was successful and their son was now a toddler. She thought of it all like a baseball game. Three strikes and you're out! Two miscarriages, and maybe one more try will prove to be the winning run. This concept fit very well in to my world. Maybe God was speaking to me through my friend. I decided once again to leave it in God's hands, and sure enough I got pregnant and this time everything was going great! I was feeling good and my heart is filled with gratitude. Now perhaps we will beat the recent odds.

What happened next in our lives does not happen to a lot of people – especially in our neck of the woods. We could never have a clue or an inkling such a thing could happen to our enchanted kingdom. Only a crystal ball would know this truth. It was July 4th, 1999 and we were visiting Steve's mom for the long holiday weekend. We got the call after church and just as we were packing the car to golf and then go for a celebratory 4th of July picnic lunch. We learned that there was a tornado in Fargo and it had hit Steve's All American Athletic club. The walls were broken, the roof had collapsed, and rain was pouring in. It doesn't sound very good at all. We packed quickly in disbelief and headed for home. Steve was a changed man. His only statement was "Oh my God. I hope that it is completely gone." Everything in our world was planned and we were especially conscious of our financial position when we elected to have our big family. The two-hour drive was very unusually quiet with no answers to the multitude of questions. Everyone we could reach said it was a terrible disaster.

Steve had devoted his entire professional career to health and wellness. The Athletic Club's success was due to his unfailing dedication to that mission. His professional dreams were one in the same, as the personal philosophy he had been living for most of his life. He never let anyone outwork him and he would never quit until he finished whatever it was he said he would do. This challenge is nothing that anyone can be prepared for. A short while later he wrote this intimate review of the experience.............

"It all started on July 4, 1999. A beautiful Sunday morning after a night of rumbling and a little rain we all got up for church and to enjoy a wonderful round of golf, a picnic, family fun and games, and the last great fireworks show of the millennia. With four sons 10 years and under, it is always a bustle around our house so it was not surprising that after our inspirational start at church we did not think to investigate the answering machine at Grandma's house. We got changed rather quickly into our favorite golf gear including Michael Jordan Chicago Bulls outfit, Tiger Woods attire and Nike's finest casual apparel—this golf outing is for a 10, 8, 6 and 2 year old boy to show off their athletic prowess.

As we backed out in our conversion van to leave Grandma in charge of preparing the picnic dinner we were surprised and quite concerned when she came sprinting out (Grandma doesn't sprint a lot). She had a scared look in her eyes and told us that there had been a terrible storm in Fargo and that our accountant left a message saying that the most valuable asset I own and the home of the business that I have built for seventeen years in order to have a stable existence had been badly beaten by a tornado ("totaled out" were the exact words).

Now, I think that I have experienced a lot of challenging things just as everyone will in their lives. I had been told at the age of three that I had a life threatening disease and that I would never live as other "normal" people do. I have experienced my son being told the same thing. I was told that because of a severe injury in the third game of the season I would not play another high school basketball game. I have been told by IRS agents that my business would be closed in three days if I did not pay them more money than I had ever had at one time in my life. I have been told by my wife that twice in one year she had lost babies as she tried to have the little girl that she has always dreamed of. I have been called and told that my dad died suddenly while my son was with him of an unexpected heart attack. I have been told for most of my professional life that I could not do what I believed was necessary because I did not have the money or support that was needed. This call once again left me filled with the questions I had been taught to ask myself for 42 years when I am tested. What does God want me to do now? How is this situation supposed to end in something good? What do I have at this time to be happy and enthusiastic about? Who will hate me or criticize my actions after I overcome another obstacle and make it into an opportunity? Haven't I had enough tests in my life already? Couldn't I just be a living example of God's will for success rather than an example of how to overcome challenge?

I have experienced questions like this before and I also know that the simple answers come to me when I (or should I say we) give them up to the hands of God so that He can lead me to His answers. There is no measurement of a problem or challenge. Each of them is either small and insignificant or large and cumbersome depending upon how we want to experience them. I have been asked numerous times why I have to work so hard at the things that I do or am involved with. I usually ask "What do you mean?" First, I believe in luck and second I believe that God has been busy planning the course that my life will take. God is too busy to make my life either easy or interesting (bad luck is the term some use). In the current case I will, in my state of wonderment and confusion, remain observant, stay optimistic (maybe my insurance will make me an instant millionaire), prepare to work smart and hard (as I try to everyday) and to continue to keep my priorities in order and to enjoy each blessing that is planned for me. Despite this, it is hard to avoid the natural tendency to get crunched up inside from taking you over. I dealt with that crunching and played mental games on my 2-hour drive home with my wonderful wife and four magnificent sons....who kept saying "This will be great Dad, now you can build that big club you've been working on!" I had been working my entire life to build a mega club and the funding letter came in a week after this disaster happened. One of the requirements was that I use the business that blew down to secure the loan...another challenge....

On the drive into our twilight zone we discussed possibilities, probabilities, necessities and perplexities as a family (it is a fond habit of ours). We joked with each other. We consoled each other and we promised each other that our love makes all of us strong enough to do anything and everything we need to do to be proud of our achievements each day. Those immediate minutes and hours following a challenging confrontation are the ones that build us up and keep us growing. If they are filled with the right thoughts and emotions as motivated by the right people and beliefs they can prepare you to face and overcome anything that gets in your way. Soon I was prepared to face my enemy with eyes and arms wide open and as we drove into Fargo, North Dakota that sunny Sunday afternoon. I realized that this would be an opportunity to grow character muscle like a lion on human growth hormone. My place of business had not been demolished which would likely have been easy to reckon with—instead, it had been bludgeoned like a warrior with a steel mallet. The roof was gone on both ends.

Trusses had been blown away. Rafters were exposed, and most of the shingles were gone. The exterior concrete cover of the building was cracked and broken. Inside there was water everywhere...walls, floors, ceilings, carpet were twisted and soaked through and through with no roof to cover them even if we dried them out. Insulation was blown out. Electrical wiring and lights were pulled out with the roof that had blown away wrecking our outside lighting and inside lighting. Our sign was broken. My health club is a service business—we can sell nothing without a place to provide service and now my place / our place / the place I had worked for seventeen years and many times 20+ hours a day to build would no longer serve my friends—the +3000 customers of The All American Athletic Club in Fargo. The walk through and around was overwhelming to say the least. How could we ever recover from this?

Now we must eat to build some strength and then we can go around and check to see if any of our other friends were badly damaged by this storm. Our drive will indicate if there are others in greater need of our help and concern than our situation demands of us. We can take care of all of our dirty work and come home for our little family Independence Day celebration. I know that I will be busy and also feel that I must be busy in order to keep my mind from becoming boggled by what my reality actually is. I have four children and my wife (recently announced pregnant) to love and care for. I have essential costs like the home mortgage, insurance payments, $22,000 in payroll on Monday, bankers who want payment, leases, repairs, 50+ hard to find, train and motivate employees, +3000 regular customers to answer to, car payments, 2 baseball teams to coach, utilities, clean-up, advertising, promises of a too long awaited family summer vacation (first ever), insurance agents to call, adjusters to argue with / if they are normal and hired by the same guys who must write the checks back to me…..and on and on—"Oh keep it simple and get busy—that's how you bring order out of chaos—act first and rely on intuition until emotions ease up and you can think clearly and orderly." Tonight is the 4th of July and it is about hope, faith, and family. Tomorrow is about business.

This family of mine becomes ever more proactive in my recovery and that transition from emotional trauma to clear and simple thought. The first step is when my 2-year-old, Chad, reminds me that he needs a new diaper….all parents who have changed one will know what I mean by "this brings you back to reality." Second, is when we get into the car and our boys are quiet and non-argumentive about where we will eat. This is a sobering experience, as it is never silent when we have discussed this subject before. We go to one of our favorite haunts, "Chilis," where everyone has a "favorite" and we are blessed by great, friendly servers and the comfort of good food. My head though, is abuzz with questions and decisions I know that I must make. I also am moderately inquisitive about how crushing this blow will be to my ability to manage the financial obligations at home and work which I must keep up...I am quietly amused by the question of who will be patient and kind and who will disinterested and aggressive. I know that I will learn who my friends are. We leave the restaurant with smiles and I am filled with confidence (perhaps temporal) that I will find guidance to master disaster just as the "Professional Wrestlers" claim to every night when I am seeking something meaningful to watch on TV.

As we head home for our Fourth of July celebration I continue to drift from my personal reality to my professional reality. I am surrounded in my personal life by people I love and respect deeply and who love and respect me. I am energized by their presence and the thoughts, words, and deeds that we share. I am fulfilled as a human being when I participate in their growth and development as human beings and more importantly as Christians. As a husband, father, son, and spiritual leader I am confident and committed in all that I say and do. In my professional life I feel insecurity, lack of energy, distrust and little respect for many of the people with whom I compete and do business. I do not know who to trust. I do not know who to have faith in. I do not know who is really as committed to me as I am always committed to them. I really am confused by whether all of my hopes and dreams for my future in the profession of health and fitness are possible, worthwhile, and valuable enough to me and the people I love to justify the pursuit of them.

We're home! We extract the world's biggest box of fireworks and everyone prepares to light up the night. Punks and fuses in three of the boys hands—my 2-year-old will have to wait until next year—and we are off into the world of thrills and spills. It's lots of fun and we incur no injuries. As much as I hoped it would happen, none of the big explosives went into those three downed evergreens in my backyard (it would have been much easier than sawing and carrying them out). We finished up our event with sparklers and a brilliant piece of reality was brought home to me when every one of my boys wrote their name with their sparkler and smiled the entire time. Isn't it great to have a name you're proud to write in the sky and a smiling face to stamp it for safe haven into the future! Those two valuable commodities (a name and a smile) are priceless riches and I promise myself not to forget that. Then we said our prayers of thanks for the day, kissed as always and my wonderful troop of enthusiastic believers and supporters were out with the lights for a wonderful night of snoozin and schmoozin with the angels of their dreams.

Now I can switch from being Dad to being husband for a bit. Ann and I have just recently found that at the ages of 42 and 39 (forever) we are expecting to have one more child. She, has had two miscarriages in the past year as we have tried to fulfill one of her dreams to have a little girl. I know that this day has been hard on her too. We visit poignantly as always about the potential pluses and minuses of our current situation and I assure her that as always I can make this work out in all of our best interest and that God gives us tests to get smarter, not to flunk us out. I really hope that her heart is filled with confidence that I can make this work and I set out on my way back to work to review the damages and layout the plan for tomorrow.

At about 11:30 pm I am at what used to be my place of business. I sit down and sort out the order of business. First, who must know immediately tomorrow. Number one—THE CUSTOMERS—who come to our door at 6 a.m. for their workout. The staff has been called by their managers and notified that, at present, everything and everyone will be going to our other business location in Moorhead, Minnesota. I write a note and tape it to the door in a temporary fashion because I do not want anyone to think that we will be closed for very long—that is not my intention. Then I make a list of everyone else needs to know. Now my must dos - 1) Survey the damage—take photos and a video.   2) Make a list of concerns.   3) Mitigate damage.   4) Review the insurance policy.   5) Find a way to cover payroll and this month's expenses.   6) Figure out how long the repair will take. 7) Figure out how to serve all of our members—pool and aquatic classes.   8) Figure out how to keep the most staff on board without going broke.   9) Minimize panic amongst the members. That is enough must do's. Now a list of how to's for me to keep in mind as I go through the next days. 1) Stay positive. 2) Look for ways to gain...honor, respect and position. 3) Never give up. 4) Remain aggressive. 5) Get what you believe is right—not what others tell you is. 6) Plan for the future—think for the future and act for the future.   7) When answers are not obvious—don't answer … take time to think and pray.

It's 3 a.m. and I know that I must rest. In order to sufficiently bore myself and get into the mood for sleep I grab the insurance policy that I know will be an important part of my next phase of life and begin to read. Once done I am really ready for bed and I am quite confident that my policy should be good enough to cover the needs that I have to successfully get out of this jam. Then I cried and asked God, "Why this, why now, why me?" "You better have a good answer for this." When that is done I do what I never forget and interestingly I thank God for every opportunity and blessing he has provided me. That's what I always do and it always reminds me of the good things and comforts me. My rule is to kiss all of my children and give them my blessing. Finally, I kiss my wife and tell her I love her—no one will ever hear that too much! There is an incredible energy derived from love and when you can build that energy with such simple and enjoyable actions why miss the opportunity. I sincerely believe that if we all do this every time we end our day, each new one will start positively and confidently for everyone we love and live with. It will change your ratios greatly!!!!! Success and Happiness overcome Failure and Disgust.

Sleep never really occurs even when your eyes are closed and you are snoring in times of extreme stress and turmoil. I know this morning that I have been in bed for a couple of hours when 6:45 am greets me on the alarm clock and I think just a couple of more minutes and roll over because what do I really have to get up for today? Most people are still on vacation—my insurance agents, my contractors, most of my customers, my bankers, half of my staff and many of my friends are gone for the 3-4 day holiday weekend. What do I do besides go in and look at all of the damage and wonder what do we do next? This isn't like me at all. I have been getting up every morning of my entire life whether after 1, 2, 3, or 4 hours of sleep and after a 20-21-22 or 23 hour working day prior I have always looked forward to having ideas, making new ideas into reality, or helping to make someone's life a little better with my handshake, smile or words of motivation and encouragement. Today I feel like I've lost "That Lovin Feelin." So I sleep until 8 am and then start on this wonderful(??) journey into a complete world of the unknown.

It's funny but at this time I really feel quite alone in my world of responsibility because it seems that no one else can really know where I am and what I am feeling. Who do I trust? Who can or will help and who will or can hurt me? Who really cares about me and my family? Who really cares about me and my business of 17 years? Have I placed myself in such a vulnerable position because of my desire to succeed or my fear of failure? If money is not important how do we survive and live a happy life without it? Do I pay my highly inflated diabetic life insurance? Do I pay mortgages? Do I pay equipment leases or do I buy clothes for my kids? Do I pay for my family's needs first or my business' needs. How far do I go into my personal savings and credit cards to keep things going? What does having Business Interruption Insurance and Building Insurance mean when you actually need it? I guess I better get to work and call my insurance agent to file the claim and find out what happens and when. I also better get there to get the phones moved to our other club and help field the questions that we know will be coming today. "Dear Lord, please bless me with the insight and leadership to know the answers, to deliver them properly and to find and recognize the steps (when I am presented with them) that will lead me to where You want me to go."

I am now at my business and it is real again today. It is a horrible place. It is all wet and smells. It is cracked and broken. Wear and tear are everywhere and are just simply overwhelming. It is insecure and even looks more worn and torn than it did yesterday. More parts and pieces have fallen in. I am continually fighting with the inconsistent desire to simultaneously laugh and cry for it is impossible to discern if this is a tragedy or an incredible joke. I think of one of my favorite songs and one that I hope someone will sing at my funeral with zest and enthusiasm "The Lord Loves a Laughing Man." I must have something to look forward to and so this must be an opportunity. I can, if I desire with the will to win, make this lemon into lemonade. I guess that my desire today is to get out of this building.

In minutes I/we lost most everything that a businessman, father, and husband and wife work long and stressful hours to accumulate to ascertain the stability of their family's future. I soon learned that insurance companies, banks, attorneys, government programs, friends, and neighbors are not the answer to life's greatest challenges. I have learned that I may never get the physical assets I had earned and the related comforts back. Yet, through the darkness, and devastation I gained richness that I could not have accomplished otherwise and that richness has prepared me for my eternal future. From that disaster, I gained unquestioning trust and faith in God's unconditional love. I had believed that I could overcome anything with God's help. I learned that God can overcome anything with my help. I thought that I had planned well enough to survive any disaster. Now I know that God has a plan to guide me through any disaster. I thought that I had all of the connections to make anything work out right for me. Now I know that God has all of the connections to make things work out right for Him. I thought that as a great leader I would succeed. Today I know that I must be a great follower to succeed. It goes on and on and it amazes me because through the confusion, trials, chaos, and fear, whether I believed it would happen or not, my prayers and our needs have been answered and my faith has grown stronger each day. God's grace and love have become the real center of my being and I have learned to be patient, faithful, and always ready to heed his direction in the belief that what I am and will be is truly determined by God and not by me. I find strength for this in 1 John 2:15-17.

My faith journey has lead me to realize that when money, time, relationships, plans, health, or happiness are messy it is important to approach every day as a new day filled with blessings. I have learned not to focus on things in my life – but instead to focus on love. I don't measure my success by looking at others – I measure success by looking inside myself. I do not take pride in influencing others – I take pride in allowing God to influence me. At the end of each day, I pray alone if necessary or with those I love. I hug and kiss them and remind them of how much both God and I love them. That is my wealth and richness!

Christian faith resulting from a financial disaster has been a great blessing in this life that has prepared me more fully for eternal life than I could ever do on my own. I have lived with the Grace of God. I have worked with Angels of God. I have felt the Love of God. I have walked through worldly challenges with God. I have heard the voice of God. I know that there is one true God and He will help all of us to change the world if we give up the pain of being "the boss" to Him. In life, it is really hard to give up control. However, when you give up control to "The Man with the Plan" the confidence, peace, joy, and energy that you get back feel really good, and that feeling will last for eternity. Jesus said it best in Matthew 5:6 "Happy are those whose greatest desire is to do what God requires; God will satisfy them fully!"

This event has changed us and our world forever. We did not only go from a very set family to a family with many questions but we went from a very solid family with plans and processes that really worked to a family with more than a million dollars in debt and no income to support it. We also had about sixty employees we both loved and cared about who were in the same boat as us. Steve had already committed to making payroll and helping them to find other opportunities until this could be fixed.

During these hard times all of us understood emotional strength is so very important in people's lives. You can read studies that prove this is real but hard to measure in detail. For people with diabetes, staying emotionally strong is a key in keeping stress and blood sugar levels where they belong. In addressing care for diabetics and in some of our other medical experiences it seems doctors can overlook these "real life" aspects of the disease. My husband has been working very hard since Eric's diagnosis to capture this lifestyle data and to make it measurable and relevant to the patient, caregiver, and the physician as a useful tool in building healthier people. Diabetic patients aren't abstract "subjects" to which the medical community should just throw new drugs and devices at. The people make the medicine work. Patients' minds and behavior matters as much as the treatment available. At this challenging time I was just beginning to understand common sense is your greatest tool for both getting through life's challenges and tests as well as in combating disease. I will become more intelligent in this knowledge as my experience grows and I have results to prove my understanding.

....

When it comes to disasters in this world I can tell you no one will ever offer too much assistance. Steve can count on both hands the people who really went out of their way to ask if he needed help. This is a guy who has helped everyone who ever asked him to. He has done charitable events for every needy group in town. He knows everyone. He has never asked for anything but has always given and offered everything. Yet, very few ever asked if he needed anything and many said no when he asked for the simplest things like extending a note or taking back leased equipment because there were no customers to use it.

Chapter Seventeen

At night while away from work, I wanted Steve's time to be stress-free and as relaxed as possible. Our business is closed and probably won't re-open where it is now. The damage is too much and the Scottsdale Insurance Company would not do anything to resolve this terrible event. They are simply starving us to death. They do not even return Steve's calls and he cannot get one bank in our community to help him restart. He has tried everything from rental to expansion but this is boom time for everyone else in the world and our business is no concern of theirs. We could not even get a roofing company or roof trusses for four months. We had thousands of active clients in this business and there is no way to salvage twenty years of work. Yet, Steve continued to find ways to keep our family financially secure. His professional life was set off course and he was trying really hard to get back on the right path.

      The journey to recovery is just beginning. We had to re-examine a lot of features of our world. Was this going to destroy my storybook life and path to happily ever after? Can it possibly work out? It seems everything we try goes nowhere. The world is too busy. The world is too happy. The world is too selfish to think a family who is always happy and fun can need support. Banks and bankers are a great mystery to me. How can they charge fees and penalties and say no to our requests when all we seek is for them to make a safe bet. We have known these people for a couple of decades and have never let them down. How can we be a bad bet when we live the American Dream – own our business, make our payments, pay our taxes and give jobs to hundreds of people? It is sad how hard it is for a hard working family to recover from disaster. I read papers and wonder at the stupidity that I am living with. As I consider it all I am reminded one of the most important elements in a fairy tale is there is always a problem that must be solved. I still believe in fairy tales. I know we will get this problem solved, and it will lead us to a deeper understanding and appreciation of the path God wants us to follow. Once again, patience, discipline, and unwavering commitment are the critical features to our happiness.

These are hard and frustrating times for both Steve and me. The bad fairies seemed to be turning our world upside down. Bill collectors are calling. Collection companies send out frightening notices demanding immediate payment, or else. We are wiping out savings and using credit cards to survive financially each month. Steve made payroll on a number of his salaried staff because he was sure he would find a way to recover and keep our business alive. Due to the dishonesty of our insurance company, attorneys, landlord, and everyone else we spent to recover when we should have saved and restarted. Steve temporarily took on some consulting gigs that helped with some of our expenses, but when would life get back to normal? At first we talked weeks, then it was months, now it is years. This unusual freak of nature (that tornado), had aggressively chosen us. What was the purpose? All I know is it did not hit and leave but instead it immediately began to shake, rattle, and roll our kingdom and now I cannot guess at when it will stop. This has truly turned into a story of make believe because I could never have written it this way.

Steve lived every day with the incredible stress of huge financial and ethical challenges. He has always had an incredible ability to land on his feet no matter how tough the challenge. He also is not the kind of person who anyone would ever know had a problem. Perhaps that makes him easier to dislike and harder to help. These challenges were all inside of him. I knew it was hard but he would never really share any of his pain or fear with any of us. He always made things work smoothly when it came to the needs of our family. He reminded us all that food, security, and love were never in shortage. His positive attitude and his confident pursuit of success kept him mentally, physically, and spiritually healthy. He would do anything for anybody – within his power – at any time. We were both raised to believe if you constantly focus on achieving the will of God on earth, He will help you accomplish all that is in His will. I heard Steve praying alone and crying at times but it has to work because there is no other option. We both prayed in our own way at our own times and for our own needs and God miraculously seemed to provide for us when the need was most urgent.

I felt guilty at times because I was a stay-at-home mom. Steve also told me that those same bankers and bill collectors gave him no respect for our decision to have a full time mother for our family. I knew my work was important and Steve supported my decision, but making some extra money for our family would also really help right now. I hemmed and hawed for a while over the going back to work dilemma but in the end the "pros" outweighed the "cons" of staying in charge of our activities and supplying the belief that nothing is bad in our world. We wisely decided to keep our lives as simple and uncomplicated regarding expenses, demands, and needs as we could. As one of my sons pointed out, one side of the dollar bill states "In God We Trust". We all had to learn to cope well with the money we had rather than worrying about the money we didn't have. Another saying that came to mind was "The first of all wealth is health." This verse helped to keep my spirits up. Even with our temporary setback, we were all 'truckin' along and we are all healthy and happy. Despite diabetes, the energy we received from our sons continued to fuel both of us positively onward.

Life has taken another curve, and through this latest detour we learned we better hold on tight to God's steering wheel and He will continue to lead us down the righteous path. At the beginning of my fifth month of this seventh pregnancy a prenatal check-up showed I had developed a condition called Placenta Previa. What in the world was this unusual condition? The baby was growing and I was feeling good. I was told the baby could come early if the placenta was ruptured. I needed to take it easy. How was I going to do this with four energetic boys at home who needed my care and attention? How could I do this when we had just lost our livelihood and security to a tornado? The doctor meant business though, and somehow I knew this was a serious situation. I had a few close calls and as of November 1, I was put on restricted bed rest for the remaining four months of my pregnancy. Steve became my fairy Godfather. He took charge of all the household chores that were a part of everyday life. He was both a dad and mom for the boys. He took them to school, church, dinner, shopping, gave baths, said prayers, tucked in and filled every gap with a smile and love. Family and friends showed their love and support during the day and we felt fortunate for all of their help. Steve's days were long, but the added responsibility didn't seem to take a toll on him at all. It was rather unusual. I knew that he slept very well – when he slept. He handled it beautifully and that display of love will be etched in my heart forever. Live like there is no tomorrow and you will never have a bad day. We lived that way and none of our days regardless of the frustrations or challenges were ever that bad. We laughed, lived, and loved so that there would never be any regrets.

Our littlest angel was born righteously right before Valentine's Day and now, finally, a princess was part of the kingdom. Four princes, and one princess. She was immediately royalty in our home. There was just something unusual about her presence. She brought a new beauty and sweetness to our kingdom. She was bringing us hope for the future. Now I felt more confident than ever that someday when I am gone my legacy will continue now that a girl was here in our family to keep the traditions going. A real bond developed right from the start between Chad and Kyrsten. He became her knight in shining armor while protecting her and watching over her at all times. She could not go anywhere without him on watch and caring sincerely for her propriety and safety. Maybe unconsciously he absorbed some of the responsibility from my shoulders. Their relationship will continue to be strong for many years to come. Our kingdom is now complete. Were we finally all getting back on the happily ever after path? What we would experience next, would cause us to search once again, for a road map with more options to get us to our destination.

Chapter Eighteen

As I have mentioned, our second son, Joran, has lived his entire life with an unusual understanding of diabetes. He knows the symptoms, the routine, and the highs and lows of the disease. He is always very inquisitive and always seems to be on top of things when it comes to Eric's life with the disease. He is titled by Steve and me as "Eric's guardian angel" – Steve more specifically calls him "the magic man" and he takes pride in those names. He too, has started playing baseball, soccer, youth football, and traveling basketball and is honored to have his dad as his coach in most of the sports. He knows even with diabetes and as "an old guy," his dad is the world's greatest coach and still a very good athlete. Joran is likely the most conscientious of all of my boys in all he does and he really strives to understand everything and to participate in making things work in the best way possible. Steve still has an envelope in his desk with about three dollars of coins from Joran (everything he had) and in that envelope it says "Dad, please use this to start building your new gym. I know it will be great." Joran brought this to his dad the day after our gym blew down. He always has an uncanny way of looking at the bright side of things.

Our household is busy and thrives with the unspoken creed being, a boy's day never ends until he drops over from exhaustion. Joran is growing up, but never seems to grow out. His metabolism is high like most kids and he eats like a horse. With the cold weather, he is fighting a case of psoriasis, the insides of his elbows are excessively dry and red all the time. He refuses to wear short-sleeved shirts, despite the fact they were the fashion for a kid of his age. His energy levels seem to be dropping off, but this seems a common trait with pre-teens. I had an unusual conversation with the lunch supervisor at his school – a neighbor - girlfriend of mine. Joran is being repeatedly reprimanded during lunch and recess over the last couple of weeks. He is being disrespectful when spoken to. His demeanor at school is kind of cranky, and sassy. These are all very uncharacteristic of Joran or anyone else in our family. Joran and I discussed the questioned behavior and we came to an understanding. He really couldn't put his finger on it, but he is going to try not to do anything that is not nice. Soon after that his days seemed to become brighter. Who knew what it was all about? His male hormones were probably flaring up.

North Dakota provides us with four seasons, but we just categorized them by the related sport or as the warm and cold seasons. Fall, winter, and spring move into cold, coldest, and then cool seasons. Summer is what we all live for! We love warm, occasionally hot, and rarely but sometimes very hot weather. Joran is excited this summer because he was invited to spend the long Fourth of July weekend with a good buddy and his family. They would be celebrating at a resort and enjoying boating, tubing, fishing, swimming, and of course eating. All of these are favorite activities for Joran. His brothers were bummed out but we all felt the adventure he could enjoy was worth the sacrifice and best wishes were sent from us. It was the first and only 4th of July we have not been together but we all wanted it to be great for him. We talked by cell phone over the weekend and when he returned we expected him to be thrilled and filled with stories. Instead, he returned exhausted, frustrated, and concerned. He had enjoyed his get away, but his conscientious and inquisitive nature caused him to return with a lot of unpleasant questions. It is a monumental question and unfortunately, he was filled with fear that he already knew the answer.

Joran began to unravel the sequence of events that led up to his questions. Throughout the weekend he constantly was stopped from enjoyment because he had to stop what he was doing and go to the bathroom. He knew it was really hot, but he was also extremely thirsty all the time. He got really unusually tired from really easy things. Fishing was the best activity because it was easy to go to the bathroom on the lake and it also required very little energy. We were all out on the porch together. There I heard a declaration of truth my ears really didn't think they would hear again nor did I think I could endure again. My second beautiful son boldly announced, "I think I need to take my blood sugar." It resonates in my ears to this day. I just keep hearing it over and over again. I had to step inside for a minute to get my wits about me. I was probably trying to avoid the inevitable answer. Once again Steve drew from his spirit of confidence and commitment to walk through the testing and comforting when the verdict was affirmed. Maybe if I didn't hear or see the answer, then it wouldn't be true. Steve said he will never forget the look on Joran's face when the glucometer read "Hi." Joran knew what that meant without any verification from his dad. His eyes looked into Steve's and there was an emptiness and the light just seemed to disappear from his whole being. Steve said it was more sad than watching someone die because in this case the pain was eternities deep and it wasn't going to go away. His body just slumped with excruciating sadness and a realized truth he was unable to hide. The man who could do anything must have an answer. Steve's only answer in that moment was to hold him and hold him and hug him there on our front step with tears streaming down his cheeks. It was as though he had let down two of the most important people in his world and could never make up the failure to either one of them.

Unfortunately, all of the smartest men in the world cannot find the answer to diabetes. He still exuded in his reaching, wishful eyes, and extremely urgent hugs that he had hope it could somehow be wrong or go away. Why couldn't his dad find the answer now both he and Eric needed to hear? Everything must somehow be made okay. The question that came to all of us was, "Is this for real? How can God allow this all to happen again?" In any moment of discovering a disease that changes your world I am sure the same question comes from the heart. None of us are born and trained to expect the unexpected and even worse to expect that our health won't be anything but perfect when we are young.

Everything seems to change so fast when something big changes. For us it seems something big happens every other month. First we lose our business to a tornado. Next I am bed ridden for months awaiting our baby and then recovery is challenging with so many children and a husband without income and instead many expenses. Now we have a second son with juvenile diabetes. A few minutes ago he was fine, now he had diabetes. All those sneaky little signs from the past few months I should have noticed may have been leading to this bizarre realization. How dumb am I? How preoccupied with life am I? Had I been putting off this news on purpose? How could we have two children with this horrid disease? A sword was piercing my heart for the second time. What was going on here anyways? Once again Steve was determined and guided by a superior power. He held him, spoke quietly and directly with him and then he immediately gave him a dose of insulin. The truth was there. An action needed to be taken. I made an appointment at the clinic for the next morning. Steve was going to make sure to minimize all of the stressful and intense methods and clinical protocols by making sure his blood sugars are normal and he has had proper insulin injections before we go to the appointment. That way we could make this entire episode as easy for Joran as possible. No more pain was needed. It has been felt by everyone and it does not need to be felt again.

We all finished out the day together. Kyrsten had fallen asleep. We put her to bed in her room. Then we put the boys to bed in their dorm style bedroom. They had double decker beds. Two sets of bunk beds for four brothers who adored each other, and when they had been given the opportunity, they all chose to stay together and share this one room. Now there would be a bunk bed for the diabetics and another for the two who had been spared. Unbelievable!

We all said prayers together as we did every other night. We thanked God for all of our many blessings. However, the normal routine seemed a little out of sync. It seemed very hard tonight, as we prayed for the guidance to help us understand this plan He had for us all. The light just didn't shine as bright tonight. My soul was dark and empty and it was hard to hide the sadness and confusion I felt deep inside. I knew I couldn't give up on Him. He was all knowing and I needed to continue trusting in Him. But why this now? Why would a loving, giving God who we relied on for guidance and leadership in order to find peace and joy do something so amazingly mean to someone who was so amazingly innocent and good. Why would we have so much uncontrollable disaster cast upon us all again?

There was a spirit in their room that night – a unique spirit. It was a spirit of sympathy, concern, fear, wonder, and love. I could tell Greg and Chad felt sorry and also fearful for their own risks. Yet, they would not disclose their fears because Eric lived with them well every day and they would never say anything to make their brothers sad. It was strange. It was an unusual atmosphere. We said our good nights, shared kisses, "I love you's" and I made my way downstairs. Steve stayed to tell his story. It would be a great one, but I knew I could not sneak and listen this time. With every step I took the sadness got more intense. Reaching the bottom step the tears finally began and I cried bitterly for most of the remainder of the evening. Once again the sadness was overwhelming. There was something so unspeakably cruel about it. My heart was broken by diabetes for the second time in seven years. I sat downstairs and tried to conjure up a way to be angry at someone or something I could attack to get even with. I wanted a way to get even for this whole scenario. I remember blaming the house, as silly as that sounds. I tried to make a connection between our present house and the one where Eric and Joran were born. If we had stayed there, then maybe they wouldn't have gotten this dreaded disease. Joran had recently spoken of Stanford University and thought it would be a good place to go to college. Now, how could that happen? Would all of his many dreams be shattered because of this news? Everything in his world had been running so smoothly. What now? He had excellent grades, wonderful friends, exceptional values and faith, and he did everything with a tremendous amount of passion. He was gifted in football, basketball, baseball, and band (to list just a few). And his big dreams were all just beginning to come true!

Then it hit me and I came to my senses. What really had changed? Joran was living a happy successful life. There had been no failures or shortfalls in his dad's life or Eric's life from diabetes. Steve is a healthy and successful person-much happier and more successful at important things than most. A great businessman, and more importantly, a kind, loving, intelligent, thoughtful, conscientious, deeply faith driven husband, father, and friend to all. Eric aspired for these same qualities. Since Eric was diagnosed we had all grown healthier and wiser. We routinely exhibited great lifestyle habits. We practiced good eating habits. We all had a disciplined awareness of good and bad foods. We all limited our sugar and salt intake. (Studies have proven a diabetic diet is the healthiest one to be on.) Wow! That is something to take note of. We strive to eat balanced and nutritious meals. We exercise and stay so physically active I do not think anyone can say they do more together as a family. To top it off, we love one another deeply and avoid stress by having fun together as a family all of the time and in every place. Come on Ann, this is not what I expected but it is okay because now Eric will share his frustrations, joys, highs and lows with two of his best friends, his dad and brother Joran and they will get it. Joran will have the same advantage – and that is exciting news! What really is going to change? Why would we let this change anything? This reality will make us all better.

Even though my revelation was exciting and hopeful, there still were some hidden cobwebs of concern that needed to surface. I couldn't just sugar coat the reality of the diagnosis forever. They all three had type 1 diabetes! A chronic disease with possible horrendous complications like kidney failure, amputation, blindness, and heart failure, just to name a few. Would they all really be able to live full and long lives? How sad and terrible would the end of their lives be? James M. Barrie who wrote the classic tale, Peter Pan, once was quoted as saying, "Every time a child says, "I don't believe in fairies," there is a fairy somewhere who falls down dead." I refused to let those poisonous negative thoughts I had been having takeover. I took control. I do believe in fairies, and more importantly, I believed in God and His miracles. I am being called to live a life of miracles and God is truly preparing me for something great. I just have to keep my heart and head open and responsive so I can figure out what that something great is. My happiness is essential to the health and happiness of our family and this is what I can control. Happiness is a decision and I have made it already. I will fill our world with unusual happiness driven by my knowledge that we are living the will of God and it is all good.

The demands and concerns of caring for two children with diabetes would occasionally send me into a frenzy. I had to learn to stop! I need to think about everything that was humming along nicely. Worrying became like a thief and would rob me of precious time and energy. Worry is such a useless waste of time. My mother-in-law pointed out Philippians 4:6 where it says "Don't worry about anything; instead, pray about everything. Tell God what you need, and thank him for all he has done." She was very wise about this and helped me greatly. I think it would be appropriate for someone to go back in history and delete the person who started worrying and created the word. It does no one any one bit of good. With both Eric and Joran managing diabetes there are some very real differences between the two. Eric still relies much more on us to help him manage things than Joran. Joran rapidly became independent when he was diagnosed and began dealing with the disease. Eric was diagnosed when he was four. We became the exclusive caregivers. Now Joran was eleven and seemed determined to handle many of the aspects of the disease on his own. Before Joran was diagnosed, I was just starting to wean myself off from certain aspects of Eric's diabetes management. Eric is thirteen and as an early teen I know he has to start taking ownership and responsibility for his diabetes care. When Joran was diagnosed, he must have had a sixth sense about this truth-probably because he watched the management rather than the illness for so many years. I wanted to control all things to make sure everything was right. As time passed I grew to understand independence is good and my desire to make everything perfect was not the best for Eric. Now Joran's approach and strong statement of being self-sufficient caused me to realize my controlling this disease for Eric was not the right thing to do. It did not take Eric long to respond to the freedom I gave to him. As a result of my sudden realization they both matured together in their understanding of the disease and the process of managing it effectively. Once again I realized how great the power of God's love is. He had timed these two terrible things to result in a positive and valuable experience for all of us.

Chapter Nineteen

$\mathcal{A}$s a responsible mom, I always felt a huge amount of pressure to be a great role model. I knew I demonstrated healthy eating habits and regular physical activity as permanent features of my existence. I still wonder if I am giving them the whole packaged deal. Was I a good listener? Did I let them talk about their disease? Did I keep a good sense of humor about the frustrations and challenges they face every day? As a caregiver of any kind, you must understand life throws you many, many surprises to create turmoil. Most of it is unexpected. Therefore, you just need to do the best you can, and that is all you have so let that be enough. You never need to feel alone. It is amazing where help can come from when you need it. It always appeared in my world when it was needed most. Once again, God truly knows what I can and cannot accomplish and He brings me the solutions I need when I really need them.

As a youngster, and I know I am dating myself, a favorite show of mine was "The Dick Van Dyke Show" and later "The Mary Tyler Moore Show." The strong female lead in both of the shows was Mary Tyler Moore. Now as an adult mother of two diabetics and wife of one I learned that she too is a type 1 diabetic. Through her celebrity she helped bring the disease into the forefront. When she spoke, people listened and she spoke from a personal platform determined to find the cure. She has been living successfully with it and wants others to be aware of the disease. This was encouraging to me as a young person who really had little connection with the disease, but I knew the purpose and believed it was inspirational to those living with the disease. As I contemplated the reasons for me to live the reality of understanding diabetes and diabetics I loved the thought of being on Mary's team. She inspired my need to share these stories as well as my commitment to build a foundation of success for my boys.

As the mom of type 1 diabetics, my ears would also perk up when I hear the names of respected entertainers and world leaders who live with the disease. I make it a point to mention these names to my boys whenever I have a chance. They are becoming leaders and stars in their world and I knew this extra inspiration and support could be appreciated and accepted by them. Some memorable type 1 diabetics are Halley Berry, MLB Pitcher Jason Johnson, Chicago Bears quarterback Jay Cutler, LA Lakers forward Adam Morrison, NY Knicks center Chris Dudley, recording artists Brett Michaels, Nick Jonas, Tommy Lee, Aretha Franklin and Elvis Presley. Other diabetics are Ty Cobb, Walt Frazier, Arthur Ashe, Smokin'Joe Frazier, Jackie Robinson, Thomas Edison, James Cagney, Drew Carey, Randy Jackson, Larry King, Sherri Sheppard, Tony Bennett, and Johnny Cash. This is a stellar list. All these individuals had dealt or were dealing with all the same issues my husband and sons are dealing with every day. It sure hadn't stifled them in any way. They had all made their dreams come true. It was a subtle reminder on my part, but oh, the power of celebrity and that feeling of personal connection. Those associations were always worth mentioning and they gave me hope all of the world was at my boys' fingertips if they wanted to reach out and stretch to attain it.

Public school systems add another interesting set of challenges and flavor to diabetes management. In order to follow the proper course of action for special health circumstances we always met with and informed the school nurse so she would be familiar with their condition. If needed she was a helpful mentor. During their junior high years, AIDS was a big issue in the media. Any mention of blood was treated as a serious and negative concern. The boys were ordered to go to the bathroom or nurse's office when taking their blood sugar or dispensing Humalog from the pen. They cooperated, but it did not seem like a risk to them so they found ways to cheat the system rather than themselves. They did not want to be different from everyone else and so they did not want to be obvious in any of their management or treatment activities. The ability to treat themselves and manage their blood sugars successfully gave them freedom, and they did not like it when rules made that freedom a headache. More headaches was never the goal.

The school day began at 8:30 a.m. and sometimes they didn't get home until around 6:00 p.m. at night. The days were long and their regular eating schedule was often irregular. They always had breakfast before school, and usually that would take them safely to lunchtime. I usually slipped a munchie in their backpack, just in case they needed something to eat. I always made sure they had glucose tablets (glorified large sweet tarts) with them and I even learned at one time Eric was selling them to his friends at a premium to make some money for his own use. Oh well, I guess making the best of a bad situation is sometimes okay. We made their teachers aware of their condition and some chose to keep some treats in their desks, just in case. What I learned as they grew is they adapt and they adapt better naturally than I do by worrying and trying to be constantly in control. Human beings are certainly capable of managing a lot of change and challenge.

Daily classwork was never a problem, because both boys were and are great students. As you might expect they are disciplined and find it easy to stay on task. They are on task 24 hours a day with diabetes, so this characteristic in both of them does not surprise me. I just pray that they do not one day just get sick and tired of it. Taking tests and the results of the timed tests with all of the stress and pressure associated with sitting for long periods and being unable to take breaks or eat a snack at the right time caused some frustrations for me-and them. When glucose levels were in the target range, the test taking was a breeze. However, when blood sugars get high or low their brains and bodies do not work as a normal child would and they would not perform as well as normal. Knowing they were good students helped us to understand when scores were good, then blood sugars were managed properly. If scores were low, then we evaluated the diabetic questions to see what needed to be addressed.

Obviously, low scores were not always diabetes related, but in most of the cases they were. Their track records nearly always showed a correlation. Only a couple of times were teachers not friendly to the issues. Classes right before and after lunch and at the end of the day were the worst. They would go low before and rise high after. Most teachers were sympathetic to this dilemma, and others were not. We never expected any special privileges and never asked. However, if test scores were used to determine final grades, then special effort was made by all of us to handle the situation the best we could. Their success in school was important to all of us and it has paid off – college grants and scholarships are irreplaceable values when you already have a lot of additional costs to fund. As a parent you should always be aware that your discipline, commitment, and help in building dynamic academic abilities and discipline in the responsibilities of education will be repaid many times when your children succeed in both school and life. The long nights reading books, talking through papers, and trying to figure out the new ways of teaching mathematics, etc. are well spent when it comes to college entrance requirements and student grant rewards. It is much easier to pay your dues early than to pay your bills late when it comes to college education.

Even though school ended at around three-o-clock there was still a lot of education and life lessons to learn. The seasonal extracurricular activities drew a lot of attention from our family. Practice and games took place on most afternoons. It was Eric and Joran's responsibility to monitor their glucose levels during the day so they were ready for the physical activity their sports required. When competing, they always wanted to stay on the same page as all other classmates. No special treatment required! They demanded this equal respect from their teammates and coaches and never expected any brownie points because they were diabetics. The coaches were always aware of their conditions. The friends never made an issue of it. The judgment usually came from adults.

During practice their physical endurance was tested. They burned a lot of energy and the sugars would be exhausted from their bodies. When this occurred, they knew to take a short break to refuel. They needed extra sugar and carbohydrates to continue with the demanding workouts. It takes only a few short minutes to pop a couple of glucose tabs and regain normal physical and mental function. Some coaches understood, while others were simply prejudiced. It seemed that they viewed it as a painful responsibility. It seemed in several instances this responsibility made my boys less valuable than other players on teams. A few coaches wanted to ignore the information. It was a responsibility they did not want. They just didn't want any more "jobs." Why should "these boys" be able to take a break right in the middle of conditioning? That's not part of the plan. Some coaches even seemed to be judgmental enough to move other players up first despite their being less talented. In a few rare instances they even took away game minutes for their untimely blood sugar monitoring during practice.

The boys always checked blood sugars before games and during breaks. If they were unable to perform and required a break they would request it. Eric was even strongly reprimanded by his basketball coach in front of the team for checking his blood sugar on the bench and at time outs during a game. It was important to him to know what his blood sugar was. The information helped give a confidence to his performance during the games. Most of the time, their game performance was exceptional and very worthy of praise. Occasionally, when their game was off, it just got checked off by the rest of the world as a bad game day. We eventually came to the conclusion that in most cases, if it was a bad game day, it was as a result of their diabetes. Stress and eating issues from the entire day could have a huge impact on performance. Stress generates a variety of problems for diabetics. It can cause fluctuations with blood sugar levels and all issues associated with this occurrence. Stress always has a way of causing a big mess and we always tried to plan and act in advance in order to prevent this from happening.

On game day a ritual needed to be followed. Eric and Joran always worked hard to control their glucose levels and the goal was always to get the glucose level just slightly on the high side of normal. They knew the physical activity would burn sugars fast and they didn't want to run out of steam before the end of the game. Coaches critiqued the players' performance and judged everyone the same. I did not expect anything special, but with all three of my sons having now become successful college athletes it would have been nice to just once hear from a coach that the boys had been great examples of managing diabetes in order to perform at their peak and in the best interest of their teammates. I am always amazed at how many of the coaches we have been associated with have so little ability to communicate praise or appreciation for the young people who look up to them, give up for them, follow them, trust them and would do anything for them. It's always nice to get some appreciation for all the long hours of time given to these coaches in their young lives. Come on coaches, get your leadership skills together and act like you are leaders rather than dictators. Praising people does one thing – it makes them perform better. As a mom, I was so proud of my boys and all young people for the effort they put into getting themselves ready for every practice and especially game days. My boys monitor their blood sugar all day. They count the carbohydrates from everything they eat and balance it all with Humalog insulin injections. They tried to minimize stress and maximize focus on the event at hand in order to perform well and compete successfully. All of this planning was crucial to their performance, but meant absolutely nothing to their friends, teammates, coaches, and spectators. It was an unusual preparation, but it was just an average day in the life of a teenage diabetic athlete. You do not need to get it but we all should. I am sure there are many people out there every day doing very special things in order to live normally and it is probably rarely acknowledged. Wouldn't it be good to simply give a little bit of recognition and credit where it is due?

In Eric's junior year this article came out about a highly publicized Division One college basketball player named Adam Morrison. He is currently an NBA player and I think as I talk about managing diabetes as a competitive athlete it is a good article to share. It is from the San Francisco Chronicle, page **A–1,** Thursday, March 23, 2006…………

He is 6 feet 8 inches tall, leads college basketball in scoring and takes the occasional syringe of insulin to his belly during timeouts to keep his blood sugar down.
Whether or not junior forward Adam Morrison leads Gonzaga to the national championship, his star-caliber play is a very public demonstration that there are virtually no limits on the potential of diabetic athletes who conscientiously treat their disease.

Morrison and his Gonzaga Bulldogs face UCLA at 6:57 Thursday night in the Oakland Regional of the NCCA Tournament.

Wherever Morrison travels these days, he brings with him a lesson in diabetes management -- educating by example about type 1 diabetes, a disease that long ago killed the children who developed it but that now can be controlled with a lifetime of medication, careful eating and self-discipline.

It is a path blazed by a handful of other world-class athletes. Gary Hall Jr., the Miami sprint swimmer who has amassed 10 Olympic medals for the United States, hopes to win more two years from now in Beijing.

"It's a testament to the breakthroughs in diabetes management," said Hall. In 2000, he won gold in the 50 meters in Sydney little more than a year after he was diagnosed with diabetes at the age of 24, and he won the 50-meter gold again in Athens four years later. "The tools to regulate and manage diabetes have improved so much," he said. "That's why you see people excelling at the top levels, like Adam."

Raised in Spokane, where tiny Gonzaga is located, Morrison developed diabetes as an eighth grader, in all likelihood inheriting the condition that killed his grandmother and afflicted his great-grandfather. type 1 diabetics such as Morrison lose their ability to produce insulin, a hormone that allows cells to process sugars from the bloodstream after a meal.

People with a normal insulin-producing islet cells in the pancreas manage their insulin levels effortlessly -- the body monitors blood sugar levels as a thermostat governs heat in a room. If blood sugar levels run high, a quick secretion of insulin shepherds the sugar into cells for processing.

In type 1 diabetes, the islet cells are killed off by the body's immune system. About 175,000 Americans under the age of 20 suffer from it.

Lacking natural insulin, type 1 diabetics must rigorously measure out the foods they eat and carefully match their consumption of carbohydrates with injections of manufactured insulin -- all the while trying to keep stable the level of dissolved sugars in their bloodstream.

"Diabetics face all kinds of crazy swings in their blood sugar," said Dr. Stephen Gitelman, director of the Pediatric Diabetes Program at UCSF. "You have to understand how to eat and how to balance your insulin."

The goal of every diabetic is to keep his or her level of blood sugar from fluctuating wildly. By measuring regularly with a handheld electronic glucose monitor, a diabetic can learn within five seconds of a pinprick test if blood sugar is too high or too low.

When blood sugar is too high, it can cause lethargy and blurred vision and lead to long-term problems such as blindness, heart disease and loss of limbs. Diabetics respond to a high blood-sugar reading by injecting a few units of insulin, which speeds up the body's ability to process those sugars.

When blood sugar is too low -- causing light-headedness that can lead to fainting, seizures, coma and death -- a snack of sweets or a drink of fruit juice can quickly restore the balance. Low blood sugar can be caused when a diabetic has not eaten enough carbohydrates or when there is too much insulin in the bloodstream.

"People with diabetes walk on a teeter-totter every day, trying to keep their blood sugar normal," said Aaron Kowalski, director of strategic research for the Juvenile Diabetes Research Foundation in New York.

High-performance athletics bring more complexity into this metabolic juggling act -- exercise itself reduces the need for insulin, but the stress and emotion of competition can boost the body's requirements for it.

For athletes such as Morrison, managing diabetes is itself as complex an art as shooting a three-pointer or running a pick-and-roll -- difficult but not impossible and impressive to watch when done well.

While most of the public attention to Morrison's diabetes focuses on his use of insulin injections to reduce his blood sugar level, during a game the most common metabolic problem he and other diabetic athletes encounter is low blood sugar -- requiring a frequent swallow of fruit juice or a nibble on a sweet.

Janet Cooper, a 28-year-old director of Bearskin Meadow Camp -- a program of the Diabetic Youth Foundation in Concord -- has lived an active life with diabetes since she was diagnosed with it 19 years ago.
"The general public does not understand what living with the condition is like," she said. "You are not given a shot or pill

once a day. You make three to five decisions every hour. It's a constant amount of work."

But with an installed insulin pump -- a cell phone-sized device that measures out insulin directly into the bloodstream -- Cooper runs an active camp in the Sequoia National Forest and runs marathons while checking her blood levels with a glucose meter on her belt.

Cooper notes that there is no cookie-cutter solution to diabetes. Each patient reacts differently to blood-level fluctuations and responds differently to sugars and insulin used to balance it. Nearly all diabetics face the problem that the symptoms of lowered blood sugar often feel similar to those of high blood sugar. Unless they check their levels with a glucose meter, they could end up treating low blood sugar as if it were high by adding more insulin -- driving blood sugar levels even lower, perhaps dangerously so.

Diabetic athletes rave about modern technology that has helped them overcome the drawbacks of their disease.
"Sixteen years ago, glucose meters took 45 seconds and a full drop of blood. Today, it takes five seconds and a pinprick," said Matt Vogel, a 30-year-old San Franciscan who has had diabetes since the age of 16. He competes in triathlons, climbs mountains and works as a sales rep for a company selling insulin pumps.

Morrison is by no means the first or only diabetic athlete to perform at the highest levels. Yale University standout Chris Dudley starred in the NBA for 16 years beginning in 1987, most of them with the Portland Trail Blazers. He came down with type 1 diabetes in 1981 as a sophomore in high school.

"Having diabetes, if you take care of it, can make you more disciplined," said Dudley. He didn't keep his diabetes hidden from his teammates, but he never injected his insulin during a game.

Stunned by his diagnosis at the age of 16, he was inspired by a hockey star, Philadelphia Flyers Hall of Famer Bobby Clarke, a diabetic who played the game with candy bars hidden in his uniform. "I figured if he can play Hall-of-Fame hockey, I can play junior varsity basketball," Dudley said. "Don't let diabetes stop you from doing whatever it is you want to do."

Today, Dudley runs a summer camp for diabetic kids and is putting his Yale economics degree to work for a new career in wealth management.

Chicago Cubs third baseman Ron Santo, who racked up 342 career home runs, broke into the majors in 1960 a year after he was diagnosed with the disease. At the time, diabetes in sports was virtually a taboo subject.

"I told the doctor for the Cubs to keep it a secret until my first All-Star Game," said Santo, now a veteran radio broadcaster for the Cubs. "I made my first All-Star Game at the age of 23. I told the organization, and then I went to the clubhouse and told the players.

Santo played through his diabetes for 15 years. "I always had my orange juice and Hershey bars," he recalled.
Diabetes management was more hit-and-miss in those days, before glucose monitoring and genetically engineered insulins. Santo eventually developed common complications of advanced juvenile diabetes -- he had a quadruple heart bypass in 1999 and since has lost both legs below the knee.
"I'm still riding my horse," he said from his Arizona home, preparing for another broadcast season. "I'm still playing golf."

....

The article hits on a lot of the points all people with diabetes deal with and it also gives hope that results from those who have succeeded in spite of it before.

I love game days despite the incredible worry that comes with them. As a parent, I am so proud of my sons and their teammates and only want the best for them. Games measure achievement and I am sure every parent in the world wants our children to perform at their best and to be successful. For parents with children that have diabetes, your child's health condition is always at the top of your mind and you know everything has to be right at any given moment in order for them to perform well. They constantly live and die by the discipline and consistency they practice in preparing for the moment. There were always stories in the media about athletes who pass out and even die on the court. Were they diabetics? Did they test their blood sugar? What was the reading? Were they physically and mentally ready to perform at their best? When their game was on, I answered with a loud cheer, when their game was off I answered with, "Was their blood sugar off?" Others could just write it off as a bad day or poor skills. Those who live with the disease always have questions when physical or mental performance is involved, and usually diabetes management is part of the problem. For that reason, the success that my diabetic boys have had in the world of sports is an amazing blessing and reward to their discipline and diligent work to be their best. They have been incredible. Both of them have lead their teams to state tournaments and gone on to play college sports. In the same way that they succeed and act responsibly and consistently they have taught their brothers and sister to live the same way. All four of my boys have competed in Minnesota State Championships for both sports and academics. They are leaders and mentors at all levels. I believe it is all tied to the determination they have as a result of learning that there are no excuses for failure but instead there are reasons for success. These boys – now I must say young men – are winners. If you are in a clutch, whether it is life, sports, faith, or friendship you can count on them to get the job done and done well. I will bet, even guarantee, if you bet on them you will be a winner too. Discipline, confidence, preparation, focus, and understanding of physical and mental acuity will make anyone a champion. People with diabetes live with this responsibility every day. The ones who win at diabetes just know how to win at life.

Pre-game meals are a tradition in the sports community. Most teams gather to satisfy their hunger for food and fellowship. Pasta was a constant staple for meals as an energy booster. I think all kids love pasta, and that includes mine. The carbohydrates in the pasta pack a powerful punch. For Eric and Joran the extra sugar in the pasta had the possibility of a knockout punch. If their blood sugar was high, the pasta held the ability to really wreck the day. Their teammates got pumped up and filled up with added energy for the game. Eric and Joran would instead run the risk their glucose level would get dangerously high and cause sluggish and tired performance. They attended the meals sometimes partaking and other times passing. They learned to take charge of their bodies. If they didn't, no one else would. Who really cares or understands outside of our family? Why should they? We need to care for ourselves and that is what we learned.

Our decisions about meals had to be flexible depending on what nourishment was needed before a game to stay in the target range. I had to get my game on when preparing their meals. If sugars were high, I knew we had to stay away from carbs. Lots of protein. If low, then we could carb it up a bit. It was tricky, yet exciting, and rewarding when I got the meal plan right. My joy for cooking was passed on to me from a long line of special women. My great grandma taught her daughter, my grandma taught my mom, and my mom taught and encouraged me. I loved cooking and the happiness I saw come from my children's faces made it more special. It seems that diabetics think of food differently than most people. Food is their lifeline. There is a selfish need because their emotions, acceptance, and success stem from their eating. I always felt the care I put into my meals was always appreciated. A "thanks mom, it was good," was always music to my ears. I always believed my diligent meal preparation was part of a designed mission I had taken on as my personal contribution to the well-being of my family and our fight against diabetes.

Chapter Twenty

We always take Eric and Joran for their diabetic check-ups at the end of summer before the new school year. I would try to schedule them at the same time. I feel that sharing this experience helps reinforce the belief they are in this disease together, with constant support of teammates. They would always have a shoulder to lean on and an ear to listen. They would always be able to share compassion and understanding for each other's lifestyle. The strong brotherly bond of love that was developed as young boys had now grown stronger than ever. They were now permanent teammates trying to win in the game of life. They share a lifetime goal of being able to remain unbeaten by potential complications that the disease could bring upon them if they did not stay at the peak of their game.

The doctor and nurses would all comment at how successfully they lived with the disease. They credit this with being very physically active. They left each appointment with a feeling of success, even though the confidence they carried in with them wouldn't accept anything but the declaration of a clean bill of health. The A1C test measures a timeline for blood sugars and tells you if you are staying consistently in a healthy range. The results of this test are sent home after the appointments and their competitive nature would even emerge as they viewed these tests. "What was your reading?" They would compare and proceed to give each other grief if they were not the best. They were both going through their teen years and their chemical and physical bodies were changing at very high rates. Both of them grew more than six inches in a very short window of time after their tenth grade year. Chemistry was doing a number on each of them both mentally and physically. These wild changes and their physical impact could make a lot of fluctuation in both blood sugar reading and the A1C results so this always had to be recognized as part of the equation for good health and performance.

Most times the A1C numbers were pretty similar. Some years Eric's would be lower, other years Joran's would. This was always a key opportunity to re-emphasize their "ownership" of the disease. We reviewed eating habits, and general issues. We discussed the correlation between weather changes and how they affected their glucose readings. Did the environment have a connection with the disease? Some mornings, depending on the weather, all three diabetics in our family had very similar changes in readings which was kind of unusual and not likely a simple chance occurrence. They were reminded once again it truly was an "aggressive" disease and they needed to take charge of it, or it would take charge of them. It was a constant fact at all times and in all places, if these boys were not on top of and in control of their illness they could become a victim to it in a flash. To this day, I do not believe they spend a waking and perhaps even a sleeping moment without being aware of this.

The boys' doctor liked to have the boys keep a running log of all glucose readings. They knew that would be beneficial in the long run but that habit never really worked for them because they tested as they felt it was needed and recording all of those details on paper was not even possible. The doctor would ask to see their logs and glucometers so they purposely did not bring them to appointments. They didn't like getting reprimanded for imperfection. They knew their readings fluctuated at times and would frustrate him as well as them. We all believed the disease revolved around so much more than just the glucose readings. Steve and I just knew as long as they were using bottles upon bottles of testing strips and counting calories while doing their shots as indicated by their many tests daily they would be as healthy as they could be.

I always say there is nothing scientific about managing blood sugar levels. There is no perfect way to always have perfect readings. I always feel it is so important to leave those hour-long appointments at the clinic on a positive note. The patients need to be aware of the physical impact of their disease. The scientific and medical part of it was what they learned there. The positive and committed attitude that drove them as they left those appointments, was more important than the test scores. They need to go back home confident and with a belief in their hearts they will continue to live successfully with the disease. Only then, will all of their dreams come true.

After each checkup we take them out for a treat. Just the four of us go. Ironically, it is usually a sweet treat reward for a good check-up. It's like kicking dirt in "The Troll's" face. We all know exams are a serious matter and a necessity. We all understand diabetes is life threatening. I never liked to dwell on that though. My defense mechanisms would kick in and I would silently remind myself it wasn't a death sentence. There was no proof they would die soon. My husband was proof of that. He would say, "I've lived a long time and I have no plans to leave in the near future." We always enjoyed this post check-up event, and in some strange way, I felt refreshed. Kind of like tapping each other on the shoulder and saying "good job." We had a good year, and we were ready to maintain the battle to conquer this disease, along with some new ammunition, one day at a time.

Joran continued to live relatively independent in monitoring and managing his diabetes. However, when it came to his inquisitive nature he became dependent on us for wisdom. After a check-up he would question the doctor's expertise. He never questioned his knowledge about the disease. He thought he was smart and respected his degree but "how can he know how we feel" was always his question? How does he know what a high or low blood sugar feels like? He really would ponder these questions. What if a diabetic doctor had diabetes? How cool would that be? He would really know how we feel. He would understand what we go through every day. He could answer a lot of my questions. He would get them all. A diabetic doctor vs. a non-diabetic doctor, as a diabetic who would you choose? His wheels were turning and he was serious about these questions. He seemed determined to study more about the disease and find some answers to these questions. Would a diabetic doctor (endocrinologist) be in his future or a scientist who discovers a cure for this disease? This was unusual for a young man his age to be thinking about. For Joran there were lots of ideas, possibilities, decisions .... and always, there were lots of dreams.

Lantus insulin became one of the new pieces of ammunition. Eric had been taking Humulin L insulin since he had been diagnosed. When he was little, we gave his daily injection in the evening before bed. Through trial and error we made a change in when it was given each day. His occasional insulin reactions were tracked back to the time the insulin was given. The Humulin L had a peaking cycle in the middle cycle. This never seemed to correspond with his sleeping cycle. Those severe drops in his blood sugar we attributed to the dosage given in the evening. Within a few months we wisely started giving his insulin in the morning with breakfast. The peaking still continued, at least the drops would occur during the daylight hours.

Joran was started on Lantus. He would take his shot with breakfast and found it to work great the entire twenty-four hours. We thought it best to switch Eric to Lantus. There was a slower release of insulin throughout the day and night. Not the extreme changes to the system. They both thrived on the Lantus and rarely experienced severe low or high blood sugar readings. It seemed to keep their glucose levels more regular in the target range. A huge weight of worry had been lifted from my shoulders with this wonderful new treatment.

Just as you need a pen to be successful at school, Eric and Joran need a Humalog pen to be successful in their everyday life. This was a new tool introduced to them by their doctor. They still needed their daily insulin injection, but now, their diet could have more variety with a lot less worry. After every meal they could count the carbs and then offset them with a relatively similar amount of insulin found in this pen. They kept it in their backpack or back pocket most of the time.

The doctor made out a prescription estimate for the time between check-ups. It covered test strips, syringes, Humalog, and Lantus . In a perfect world this would successfully cover the time between check-ups. Every diabetic patient is unique and obviously has different needs. Some days the boys check their blood sugar four times, others six, or eight, or whatever. Some days they need to take more Humalog, some days less, depending on what they are eating and how active they are. Prescribing amounts of supplies isn't a perfect science, especially as growing teenage boys. Supplies would run out and refills were needed. It could be a hassle to get these filled without a real, genuine, original prescription. The doctor would need to be called and at unusual times he wasn't available. It was sometimes a long and frustrating process and most times it was in kind of an emergency, like weekends or holidays, when they did not think about running low. When you are out of insulin you need insulin and you need it pronto. Steve just simply would blow gaskets when a pharmacist would tell him they needed to renew a prescription in order to fill a need. Not only was the fact and demands of diabetes enough for an innocent person to manage every day – then the medical profession had to demand more time, energy, frustration and challenge to just get the substance that gives life. He cannot understand any reason why a diabetic should need more than one prescription. It is not something you grow out of or are suddenly cured from. An insulin dependent diabetic takes insulin every day whether they want to or not from the day they are diagnosed until they die or have a transplant. What is up with renewing prescriptions? I cannot answer this one. Can anyone who lives with diabetes?

Skip forward for just a moment. When the boys left for college this issue of diabetes presented other challenges. First off it does not seem fair to burden them with the cost. For some reason there is no way to get student loans to help offset this cost. In the 70's there were scholarships that diabetics could qualify for in order to make cost management for diabetes more affordable – a well-controlled patient costs everyone less so why not help be well controlled? When they ran into dilemmas and tried to settle them alone it was always a nightmare. These are diabetics right? During these episodes I was reminded again diabetes surely remains a greedy disease because of its time demands and related costs. Monthly supplies for three diabetics totaled around five hundred dollars out of pocket and that was not including health insurance, check-ups or other related costs. We calculate the cumulative monthly cost is nearly $2,000 just for normal healthcare. Any special issues just pushed that figure up. If insulin was needed after drugstore hours when they could not reach our insurance company we would have to purchase it at the clinic/hospital pharmacy for full price which is unbelievably high for a product that probably costs a couple of cents to produce. With diabetes you have to stay on top of your game all of the time. You cannot get supplies early because they only allow you so much in a given amount of time. You have to watch the window and act in perfect step with "The system-Your insurer's system." Otherwise you pay at a premium in all ways.

Eric and Joran are experiencing both the rewards and challenges that occur during these special school years. With independence comes responsibility and it was a joy to see how successfully this was working hand in hand for them. They had been forced to learn all about responsibility for themselves at a very young age. When diagnosed as diabetics the carefree childhood existence they had known was gone forever and replaced by the harsh, "in your face" reality of constantly being in charge of every action they take. Many of their peers are experiencing personal responsibility for the first time. My boys are the definition of personal responsibility.

I remember the excitement and pride they felt when they passed their driving test. They now had their driver's license, and this milestone brings new challenges for everyone but especially for us. They have a new independence and need to understand the privileges that come with it. The apron string between us is severed a bit. Steve and I took this opportunity to reinforce lifestyle habits that must continue now, even without our constant supervision. They now did not just have a liability to themselves while driving but also to everyone else who would be trusting them to be safe and in control when they got in the driver's seat. This responsibility is one of life and death because leaving a game, or test, movie or a college party without all of one's physical and mental senses could in a simple moment end a life or change one so dramatically it would be unforgettable.

Driving rules must be initiated. General driving requirements were reviewed by teachers but diabetic driving responsibilities are demanded from us. They know they must never drive with a low blood sugar. Always test your blood sugar before driving. Always carry along carbs, in case you feel low. Never fail to stop if you feel unusual. When on a long trip, stop and check blood glucose every 45 minutes. Just as a person should request a designated driver if they have had too much alcohol, they too should request one if their sugar drops too low. Safety and prevention are what we hoped to instill in them and they are bright and responsible guys so we are confident in their safety and caution as diabetics and human beings.

The cell phone became a necessity and a stable bridge of love between the boys and us. The cell phone serves us incredibly for all kinds of communications. They agreed to always answer their phones. If they could not answer for some reason, then a text was expected. Diabetes and keeping the lines of communication open is a vital partnership. They respected our rule and it has never become an issue. Those open lines of communications have allowed me to sleep at night and also to live through some of my difficult days.

I remember reading that the rigors of managing diabetes could be stressful and lead to symptoms of depression. They said as teenagers grow, they need a lot of sleep. They can worry about a lot of issues like grades at school, friendships, girls, sports, and the constant reminder having to deal daily with controlling the disease. The sensitivity to these issues could cause blood sugars to fluctuate. These concerns always troubled me. My goal was always to bring as much joy to my children's lives as I could. Would this disease have the power to cause depression with my boys? With this awareness came concern, but from what I was observing it didn't cause me to worry. It just made me more conscious to continue staying involved in their lives. This all reinforced and reminded me of what I had always known. I will always be here for them whenever they need me.

As I grow older, and wiser I realize more clearly the limitations of human happiness. Real and abiding pleasure in life comes from giving to other people. Therefore, I have tried to teach my family you might not be happy every second of every day and that is normal. Find your joy in sharing your love with others. Make your goal to bring a smile to someone else's face. Only then will you experience and feel real joy. Always treasure those moments of pure joy. The easy way to accomplish this is to follow Luke 6:31 where it states, "Do to others as you would have them do to you." When we live with this rule in our hearts, the world around us changes at the same time as the soul within us.

Chapter Twenty One

Communication with the outside world about the disease was sometimes very difficult for me. I would have to remind myself the world wasn't going to stop just because my child had diabetes. I felt it was important for me to bring awareness into the world. I knew I couldn't change reality, but somehow I wanted to change the way other people's eyes saw an unhealthy child's reality. There are so many chronic diseases and most people have no clue about the kind of life children with them live each day. There is so much apathy and ignorance. How can it change? God made us all in the likeness of Him. He gave us all special gifts, and even my diabetic sons deserve respect when they share their gifts with the world. I quote from Matthew 7: 1-2 "Do not judge, or you too will be judged. For in the same way you judge others, you will be judged, and with the measure you use, it will be measured to you." We all have failings and weaknesses. What good does it do to criticize or take pleasure in other's hardships? A happy forgiving heart will go far in making your life and our world a much better and more fun place to live. I live it in my house and with my family and I can guarantee it leads to a healthy and healing spirit. If you do not act as a judge there is no guilt and then forgiveness is easy. Take a minute to think about it and then give it a try. You will not be disappointed.

I have three personal stories to share that reaffirmed my belief that when it came to diabetes, or any chronic disease, many people would rather practice ignorance and distance than engage and care enough to adapt. There is a deep lack of understanding and compassion given to people with a chronic illness. Who helps a person with asthma? Who gives a second thought about someone with arthritis? Who really cares about someone with a learning disorder. When was the last time you got up in the morning and asked yourself, "What can I do to help someone who has special challenges today?" I have decided to constantly remind my children everyone is just trying to get through each day the best they can. Give them a break or even better – give them a hand.

Eric and Joran attended a huge number of basketball and baseball tournaments and camps and many of them were away from home. They all worked out fine but not without added pressure and worry for me. One that comes to mind was a mandatory high school varsity team building basketball trip in western North Dakota in a town called Riverdale, North Dakota. A main objective of the trip was to strengthen the team relationships and skills by getting away from any distractions and instead focusing on communicating with each other and to building understanding and loyalty as teammates. What a great idea. There would be another team from the other side of our state there and they would scrimmage against each other and do drills with each other.

What I found out next wasn't such a great idea, at least not for Eric. This team building was taking place in a secluded town of 200 people and they could not take cell phones or be connected by phones. They would sleep on floors in sleeping bags in an empty school. The meals were being brought in for them and there was not even a pop machine in the facility. Everything closed there at 7 or 8 pm and I am not really sure where the coaches were staying. Eric sprained his ankle a week before and of course, there would be no trainer and we did not know if ice would be handy. Eric never complained about anything but we were concerned.

What if he had an insulin reaction? How would anyone know and how would help get to him there? We did find out the coaches had their phones in case of any emergency. But we did not know how they would be connected with the kids. At least there would be a way to connect if the need became obvious. What started out as an innocent, laid back, team-building event by the coaches, turned out to be a major concern and worry for me. Maybe we were the only ones concerned, but Eric was a team member and his well-being was as important and significant as anyone else on the team. He also was an important member of the team as a 6'5" shooting guard he made major contributions to any team's success just as he did in his college career as an All-Conference freshman basketball player. When coaches make decisions they need to take into account all of the players and address special circumstances directly. It happens everywhere else in the world.

Another experience I will never forget was at the end of Eric's high school career. After a family vote, we moved to a new town for his senior year. He had to take on another challenge of proving himself as a leader and athlete with only nine months to fit into another world filled with a pretty fixed social environment and expectations. He did great! With only ten days of notice he decided he would drive 70 miles each day to attend football practices until we moved. He got up an hour before everyone else and made the drive to early morning practices and managed all of his diabetic requirements perfectly. As you might guess the coaching staff was slow to recognize his incredible strength and athleticism but by the end of the season he was starting kicker and wide receiver. In the section championship game he made a remarkable pass reception that lead us to the state football tournament and it was a great way to roll into his favorite sport – basketball.

He had an incredible season on the basketball court. He earned many accolades both offensively and defensively. He was one of the leading scorers in Minnesota at mid-season. His team was rated at the top of the state rankings in our division and motel rooms were already being booked, anticipating another state tourney trip. This was a dream season as we won one game after another by huge margins. He was a double-double guy and was in the top ten scorers in our state for a major part of the season. We had only one loss (probably because coach benched Eric for not rebounding every stupid shot other players missed). I am certain that he did not like things about Eric's success as well as the attention to diabetes management. With only four games left in the season and leading by double digits we were confronted with a fluky turn of events and it changed everything.

Eric went up for a driving layup and something popped in his leg for some unknown reason when he landed. He could not walk and was obviously suffering from a sprained-or worse- ankle. Steve would not take any chances and wanted that state tournament trip as bad if not worse than anyone. He had been denied a happy ending to his high school career because of badly torn ligaments in his senior season. He rushed Eric to the emergency room and after an x-ray and exam it was determined Eric had not suffered a break. The physician recommended he come back on the next day after the radiologist had checked it to confirm his diagnosis. Because we wanted to fix it fast we scheduled his visit with the best private orthopedic clinic in the region. They reviewed the injury and the x-rays and determined he had suffered a deep tissue bruise (compartmental syndrome). They guaranteed he would be ready to go in 7-10 days.

We did everything to make this healing happen as fast as possible. We drove every day for rehabilitation. We drove more than 200 miles to see a highly recommended healing massage therapist. Eric did electric stimulation. He did cold whirlpools. He had massage therapy and he took supplements and anti-inflammatories to hurry the recovery. We had only three games left. After trying and suffering through every different sure-fire treatment we could find, and another lost game his coach emailed Steve and said he was angry because he did not think Eric really wanted to play that badly because he should be able to overcome the pain and get back in action. He said that all Eric wanted was to move here to get publicity for his basketball skills and get a college scholarship. It was so ridiculous we could not believe it. it was also from the guy who told our second son Joran that he should be playing varsity but would have to start the season at JV because the local boosters would not like both boys on the team right away. Joran was buried on JV and never made the varsity for even one game. This was all ridiculous and unacceptable but also unavoidable. We got by the first round playoff game against the bottom seed and now Eric had to play in the next playoff game, whether he was well or not. This game was against perhaps our biggest basketball rival and when Eric was healthy we had beaten them by more than 20 points. They are a constant challenger in the Minnesota state tourney and just had a tradition of being great tourney competitors.

No one could seem to figure out why Eric was not feeling better and healing faster. In my mind I wondered if it could be his diabetes. No one gave any answers. All of the medical experts just kept treating him for the same injury and then began telling us it can be a tough and timely recovery. He was having chiropractic treatments and deep tissue massage – with the tiny little metal instruments - along with the rehabilitation. On the night of the game they brought a stationary bike for him to ride instead of running to warm up. They also wanted him to keep moving on it if he was out of the game so the injury would not tighten up. Dennis Rodman was famous for riding an exercise bike when he was out of games so we bought into the theory. This was certainly not any fun on a very high-pressure game day which was the consummation of a 12 year focus on being a great basketball player who could lead his team to a state championship. Before the game he had a chiropractic deep tissue treatment – you could hear the cracking of the tissue when the tools were pushed hard - rode the stationary bike, and at halftime got a chiropractor treatment to loosen up his leg again. He played his heart out with an incredible performance despite not having played for a little more than three weeks. He lead his team with seventeen points, seven rebounds, and three steals while playing half the game but the team came up short by just a couple points.

In the finishing seconds of the game his whole being suddenly deflated and I could feel and see the tears that came to his eyes and the brokenness that was evident in his heart. The one thing he struggled to control for his entire life had caused him to fail unfairly. His physical health had prohibited him from accomplishing the goals he had so clearly proven he could achieve up until his injury. For some reason our coaches and players all ignored him as he shuffled his aching leg to the end of the stadium and down the stairs to the locker room. The rest of the players exchanged handshakes, but Eric was gone. I sat and watched and wondered what to do but it was not my place to charge into the locker room. Apparently his actions were such a big deal to some people in the crowd it became a major issue and he was deemed unsportsmanlike and criticized for his behavior. I was puzzled and had no concrete explanation. He is a quiet, straight arrow kid who has played in tournaments from Montana to Kentucky and with kids from across the region. He is highly competitive but not a bad sport. He likes the kids that just beat us and has known many of them since they were little boys. He gets along with everyone and so this hurt me, but even more it broke my heart because of how it hurt him. No one ever asked why the coaches grabbed the kids that they loved and ignored the one that got them where they were all year long.

As soon as he returned from the locker room I knew the problem. His blood sugar was 40mg/dl. The pressure and physical demand of playing on one leg had paid a toll on him. Weeks later after our insurance would not reimburse us for more physical therapy they recommended an MRI. Much to our disappointment we learned he had played on a broken leg that was misdiagnosed. We had spent thousands of dollars, been accused of not caring about the team, being bad sports and many other things and here the doctors we trusted so openly had caused all of this pain. The chiropractor and all the treatments were keeping the leg broken – they were rebreaking it. What a shame. The doctors had screwed up so many things beyond their diagnosis. We all know that they were not going to publish an apology and neither did any of them say sorry as we went through healing of the broken bone.

The incorrect diagnosis was shameful on the part of the doctors but what transpired from that game was shameful for all of us. Our basketball community shunned Eric. He was ignored for scholarships at school. He was denied a conference MVP title he was certainly entitled to. Looking in from the outside his one-time action was viewed as an embarrassment to the community. Did anyone ask why or find out what the conditions truly were? Now just wait a minute. The reason he left for the locker room was unusual, yet explainable. Here he had played an entire game on a broken leg with a lot of pressure riding on him to play his best and perform at a high level. Stress was occupying his whole being playing for a coach who told him that he did not care enough to play and as the game came to an end his blood sugar had dropped into a dangerous level. He went to his locker to get sugar and he came back when it was better.

Not one of our three coaches even reached out to him or looked out for him in consolation. One of them was too busy eating popcorn on the bench during the game. Eric's brain had started to shut down and confusion was evident. He didn't know where he was by the end of the game. Where was one of the coaches to help and lead him in the right direction? If they saw this going on why didn't they step in? They were all too busy thinking of excuses and who to blame. Not one of them ever stepped up in his defense and not once did anyone ask about it or defend him. He was branded and judged unfairly that night as being a bad kid. No one took time to try to make sense of this behavior. No one took time to understand the cause. No one said a bad thing about the incompetency of the physicians. No one mentioned the failure of his coaches. NO ONE DEFENDED ERIC.

It took me a long time to get over this. I had to learn to ignore ignorance. Our team at home (our family) all knew the truth and that's what really mattered. We loved Eric and he felt secure in that love. We all moved on and chalked it up to another diabetic misunderstanding. Our "ignorant chalkboard "was pretty big and through the years we had really filled it up. There was still some room, and I guess that was okay, because there would be many more episodes worthy of being added to that board in the years to come. Still, the unusual blessing was this particular experience and all of the inner suffering Eric felt from it probably drove him to score 40 points in his ninth college basketball game as a freshman and to earn two Player of the Week and All-Conference honors that same year. To this day I do not think anyone can intimidate Eric at anything.

Another unforgettable story of ignorance and disappointment occurred during Joran's senior year. He had been primarily ignored for the year following Eric's graduation. When his senior year came he too was having a stellar season on the basketball court after leading his baseball team as a junior to a third place finish in the MN State High School baseball tournament. This bizarre moment occurred on Senior Recognition Night for the basketball team. The coach took time to make a short comment about each senior and Joran was first. I think he was trying to be funny. He failed miserably and so I quote "I'm glad he is a senior so I won't have to be grossed out anymore watching him test his blood sugar and take shots." Waiting for laughter in response to his inconsiderate joke, the place was silent and Steve and I were numb. What did we just hear? Why did we just hear it? What an absolute idiot. My heart ached for Joran, and yet, he just brushed it off and moved on with the game that he too loves to play and is very good at. He does not need more love because he has a lot at all times. Instead he took the treatment and insults to drive him to be real good at other things. Today Joran is an academic All-Conference college pitcher in pre-med. He maintains an "A" grade point average while playing ball, working a job, and taking the required and very challenging pre-med science classes. Once again, blessed with commitment and discipline learned from the lessons he learned while growing up as a diabetic.

For most of his high school career, Joran's basketball skills and abilities were ignored by the same coach who judged Eric as not caring enough to play. Joran would adamantly defend this coach with his dad at home when Steve openly discussed his inconsistent performance, communications, and fallible notions of good basketball. He deserved at least the same respect and praise given to other players, instead of ridicule and embarrassment. Comments like this from leaders are neither funny nor respectable. This experience joined my list on the "ignorant chalkboard" that always seems to grow longer and longer. How many more could there be? Unfortunately, I'm afraid the list will just continue to go on, and on, and on…

Chapter Twenty Two

*O*ur family's life journey has taken some unfamiliar and unusual turns, and every new challenge and adventure is filled with both joys and disappointments. My life plan says it is time for us to quit exploring, put the road map back in the glove compartment, get our life into the cruise mode. Because of the boys diabetes, and Steve's twenty-year career teaching and promoting health and fitness, he has put blood, sweat, tears, and a lot of capital into a cloud-based health, wellness, and medical compliance SAAS he is very excited about. He has been on a non-stop mission to procure investors and bring it to market. Ever since the day he figured out that people would buy unique things that they wanted and needed he has been one true entrepreneur who is "living the dream" in all of its gory glory. Monthly paychecks are not part of this world. In the words of pioneers, "We eat what he kills." Instead of living month-to-month we lived on a little bit here and a little bit there. All of our income is derived from consulting contracts and investor support to get his program researched, developed, tested, proven, marketed, and monetized. He is and has always been the sole breadwinner for our family and the requirements of our life mean he works long hours with dedicated energy, positive enthusiasm, and the stamina to always find a way.

There are times when my patience with this enterprise is unbelievably strained and tested. It always seemed there are highs when everything is ready to happen. On the other hand, there are times when I questioned his technology dreams and all of the insecurities I have to live with every day. It caused arguments and stress between us. We had our house payments, monthly diabetic supplies for three people, (the supplies' total was comparable to our house payment), self-employed health insurance, living expenses for seven people, current and outstanding bills that existed from all of our personal guarantees for business loans, leases and other obligations that resulted from the tornado fiasco (we paid back more than $400,000 in expenses rather than claim bankruptcy because I did not want my family to be embarrassed at our failing to be accountable), and there were never ending unexpected expenses. All of this added up each month. He sensed my concern and would let me vent as I needed to. He never gives up though on anything that is related to our family or the inspirations he believes God has called him to serve.

He is a good listener and did understand my confusion. He would take me back to the beginning of our courtship. He reminded me he always has believed he was born to be a creator and to make a difference. So many people had told him he would be a lousy employee and in reality who hires a 45 year-old diabetic. Since our well planned business and stable lifestyle was suddenly taken from us by Mother Nature he seemed to lack a confidence his plans really made a difference. He has become more spiritual and committed to following the path that is driven by inspiration and opportunity instead of by his decisions. He chooses his destiny from the options that arise. He believes every day when he commits himself to the will of God then he is doing the right thing. He is always inspired by things that are helpful to others and so we live as a result of service. Hey, isn't that what I always wanted? We had always told our children to dream big and follow their hearts. If they work hard, and keep believing, their dreams really will come true. Why would I squelch our commitment and dreams now? Eugene O'Neill once said, "Obsessed by a fairy tale, we spend our lives searching for a magic door and a lost kingdom of peace." Why not keep searching? Aren't we entitled to try? People around us may think we are naïve, irresponsible, or that we should just get real. One time my brother said Steve should go get a job at the Walmart checkout line but instead he helped sell some banks. That is not the feedback to give to someone who is working so hard to do great things. I certainly did not approve of that attitude and it made me even more committed to achieving our happy ending. For us, life is real every day. And to date as I evaluate and consider all things it has truly been really good!

As happens in so many times of need I was blessed with the perfect inspiration concerning people who follow their dreams. It is a writing from a book called "Simple Abundance: A Daybook of Comfort and Joy" by Sarah Ban Breathnach. It says –

"Remember, before anything exists on earth, it exists fully formed in Spirit. The Great Creator does not play favorites; each of us came into being to carry on the re-creation of the world throughout gifts.

And while you are offered many dizzying opportunities in a lifetime, Spirit only comes once for each Work seeking creative expression through you, then moves on. The bottom line is that the Work must be brought forth. If you do not do it, someone else will. So when the great idea flashes across your mind surrounded by Light, pay attention! Once it exists in your mind, realize that other brain waves will be able to pick up the creative energy pattern if they are receptive. Think of your mind as a satellite dish. Creative celestial messages are continuously being transmitted. The frequency is jammed----privy to your soul only---for the infinitesimal, propriety moment. Just long enough for you to lift up our heart, accept the assignment, and give thanks.

Is the idea absolutely fabulous? Can you see it completely finished in your mind's eye? Does it take your breath away? Novelist Gail Godwin tells us that "Some things…arrive in their own, mysterious hour, on their own terms and not yours, to be seized or relinquished forever."

So for God's sake---and your own---just say "Yes."

After reading this I felt a true ah-ha moment and it was almost scary. How many of us miss our callings and opportunities because we are too busy being busy every day?

Could it be true we are all called to greatness but ignore that calling as being arrogant or ridiculous? Because of Steve and because of his belief he has taught all of us we should and can follow the will of God and pursue our special callings. Since I have come to that realization the criticism of my doubting friends and family no longer can raise doubt in me. I quote from John 20:29 "Jesus said unto him, Thomas, because you have seen me, you have believed: blessed are they that have not seen, and yet have believed." It is hard to imagine a more fulfilling life than one dedicated to serving a personal call from God.

Just like fairy tales, symbols are found everywhere. One of my favorite symbols for succeeding in my life quest are feathers. There is always opportunity for feathers to show up in random places. Birds are wild and free and have the ability to fly above the earth and look down on us and everything around us without being affected by it. I have found it mystical in how in the strangest places and at the strangest times feathers show up for me. Three of my boys and I have read a book called "The Dream Giver" by Bruce Wilkinson. At a very low time after the tornado disaster Steve was really suffering and worried about what he was doing in seeking to create a major medical technology with no money, no staff, and no ability to write code. He ran into an old friend who Steve had trained, motivated, and employed until this young man had left in pursuit of his own dreams. When Steve shared his story the friend told him he should read this book. Steve went to Barnes and Noble and because he did not know where he was going or what he was doing he read the whole book while he sat on a chair at the end of the aisle where he found the book. He bought six copies of the book that he still shares with friends in need today and he also gave us copies to read. In the book the feather represents the pen that is given to the man named "Ordinary" to use for the purpose of remembering "The Truth." Since that day, when I/we see a feather we keep them because they so often come to us at times when we need to be reminded of what our truth is. Love, laugh, and live each day in pursuit of God's will.

Steve has coached more than a thousand sports games and he also named the boys' teams the Eagles. All of the teams were extremely successful and they also seemed unusually blessed by the spiritual connection between the players. Our Eagles and "The Dream Giver" make me see feathers as a reminder of my destiny to be more than ordinary and to live in an extraordinary way. A poster I keep up and displayed downstairs at our house says, God wants more for your life than "fine." Be an eagle, not a duck. When times get tough, negative messages are received, or hopeless doubt overshadows all optimism, a feather might appear. We collect them and then find them in various places around our house, car, garage and yard. Those feathers are always signs from God to keep believing, going, and never give up. By just using simple little symbols-reminders like this it has made it possible for us to .... Just keep on flying!

Our family enthusiastically shares our lives together. We suffer together, celebrate together, worry together, and dream together. As we nurture one another other along the way we began to understand the excessive and magnificent gift we all have been given. We know we are a family filled with love and understanding, faith, and passion who would never ever walk alone no matter where we are or what we are doing. Perhaps the diabetes that lives within our kingdom is really a gift from God. God has given us many blessings. We have always faithfully understood the responsibility God has given us in raising our children. We have always taken it seriously and respected our calling as parents. I know now this disease, its requirements, and the challenge to overcome it are a blessing – the blessing has made all of us different and better than we could ever have been without it.

I remember a friend who told me our children are not really ours, they are God's. I was the one who had given birth to them all, but God had placed them in my womb. They were created by God in His image, and they were meant to serve His purposes in this world and the next. I always felt empowered, responsible, and privileged to be able to help prepare them to carry out His will in His way. I have the opportunity to raise my children with the consummate goal of ultimately serving and pleasing God. Every child is born for a reason, there are no mistakes. Was the diabetes just a fluke mistake, or part of the plan all along? Open Sesame! I needed to open myself up and contemplate this new and inspirational discovery in my world. I have a plaque in my bedroom that was given to me by a special little friend from Sunday School, and it reads, "May you trust God that you are exactly where you are meant to be." This life I live then is the plan for me and my life all along! Why did I spend so many years of my life thinking I was in control and I wanted certain things at certain times and in certain ways? This life-my life-our life is exceptional. It is spiritual. It is universal. Most important it is eternal. Thank you God!

Chapter Twenty Three

Eric finished high school with honors in his academics and athletic endeavors. He had been recruited by Coach Barry Wohler, and would play basketball at Hamline University. After researching the university and its educational benefits, he agreed to the acceptance letter and was excited about this new chapter in his life. I remember people asking how I felt about our first son going off to college. His excitement fueled mine, but my mom feelings were mixed with lots of emotion. I was not naïve, I knew the dynamics in our kingdom would change, but that was not necessarily going to be a bad thing. It will just be a new thing. Moreover, after we adjust to Eric being gone, this will turn out to be a good thing for all of us. Eric is ready to be his own man and I believe he will be a great man. As a parent we can only build a proper foundation within our children to prepare them for the many storms they will need to withstand. Eric is well built and I have no worries about his resilience, intelligence, and confident personality. He is though, the highly respected and loved brother of four siblings and we will need to give them means to maintain their uncommon unity.

Then, only a couple of months after committing to play basketball for a coach he was excited to know and play for, he received a disappointing call. It came at the end of June. Eric looked shocked when he came to tell us the news. Coach Wohler is leaving Hamline and will go to coach at a suburban Minneapolis high school. It did not seem possible. We were so excited and Eric was so excited about coach Wohler. As a player with diabetes he wanted to make sure that his coach would have no misgivings about the issues related to managing it while playing. Now the verdict was out and it was really too late to change plans. He will roll with it and we will pray the new leader will be open to a unique coaching responsibility and the ensuing opportunity –

to coach our talented son. Eric is a winner – trained and tried, emotionally, physically and statistically – a winner who will lead others to win. All we ask and pray for is respect and a fair opportunity.

Steve and I have been living under one roof for many years with five children. As a full time mom - profession as activities director - for our family I have been in charge of knowing every family member's daily schedule and all that that involved. With Eric leaving my nest I will put my trust in God, that He will watch over him and keep him safe. I know I raised him with all the right tools. My greatest prayer is that he knows how to live safely and independently with diabetes. I know when you have given your heart, energy, mind, time, love and grace every day to do your job well that when it is done you have to say "It is good." That is what I did. Now it is up to him.

Both Eric and Joran have grown into very wise young men. Up to this time, the doctor and we, as parents, have delivered all of the resources and answers to questions concerning the disease. Now the internet is available and it opens up a completely new world for these boys. They can stay educated on their own from just about anywhere if they really want to be ahead of their game. This new age of communication and information also helps with staying connected. With email, Facebook, cell phones, and texting, he will never be too far away. It is time to give him wings and let him fly. Worrying about the future could rob me of the present moment and all of the joy that was coming for Eric. Believe me, saying goodbye is not easy, but I am confident and assured by the peace I am given, that it is time to get him settled at school. I just absolutely need to meet his new roommate. He will be the unexpected receiver of membership in the long list of good fairies from Eric's past. I just hope that he is prepared for this.

When we went to his "new home away from home" we met his new college roommate and were very surprised and pleased. Eric knew that we were waiting and so Eric told him that he was a diabetic. I waited for the nervous shock in his roommate's eyes and the silence, but neither surfaced. It did not seem to faze him much. Instead, he shared that his dad was also a diabetic and that he is familiar with the disease. Inside myself, I yelled out, "Praise the Lord." God had given us another gift, and we were thankful. He can recognize signs of highs and lows and would know what to do in either case and that is real helpful to know. We contacted the Student Health Center, just in case. Little did we know that a "just in case" would present itself in his future and they would be needed and greatly appreciated.

Eric thrived at college and separation got easier with time. Our whole family felt the loss. It was very quiet when we all left Eric behind for the very first time. It was also very sullen that night when we all got home and gathered to say our nightly prayers. Joran, though stepped in as the eldest brother very well. All of the kids will get busy and they will quickly adapt to digital visits to replace their interaction with their oldest brother. For every parent of a college student it has to be different because there is always a - letting go/letting grow - dynamic that goes on. For the parent of a child with diabetes there is a keener sense of this separation. There is more of a - letting go/ letting grow/ letting him watch over his disease to stay healthy and alive - as I let go of that daily responsibility. Now it is no longer the responsibility given to me when he was diagnosed but instead it is time to let God and his guardian angels guide and continually watch over him. Sending my diabetic son alone, out into the real world, definitely had its psychological challenges. I have some heartwarming/heartbreaking stories from college to share.

As Eric adapted and we adapted he was enjoying life and his accomplishments while keeping his diabetes controlled. On one occasion in his first semester, the basketball team went for a couple of nights to a tournament.

The afternoon they were leaving Eric was on his way to pick up some essentials for the trip and he was hit by a foreign lady who totaled his car out. After some chaos and fast work with Dad on that sacred cell phone, he ended up making it home and rushing to make it to the bus on time. After checking into the hotel, Eric realized that he had forgotten his insulin at the dorm that was about 300 miles away. He did not want to be a hassle to the new coach or team and so he went to the concierge to find out there was a clinic where he should be able to get his insulin.

He did not know the city at all but felt compelled to work this headache out on his own. As you know he has been taught to be independent and never wants diabetes to interfere or affect life. He told his roommate he was going to get the insulin he needed and would return soon. He hailed a cab and when Eric got to the clinic in Wisconsin Dells, Wisconsin he told them he was diabetic and needed insulin. He presented his ID's – driver's license/student ID/insurance number - and the nurse in charge forced him to undergo a full examination before he could be provided with the insulin. As most of you probably know, time in the world of medicine has nothing in common with the rest of the world. No matter how simple the request or discussion, it is done at the care provider's discretion and with no consideration for the patient's schedule. This simple process of getting a vial of insulin took a couple of hours from start to finish. He could not call anyone because he left his phone at the motel thinking it would only take minutes. He did not have any of the players' or coaches' numbers memorized to call from the clinic. It cost us nearly $500 for this unneeded exam and when he rushed back to the motel he had missed the team meeting for his first tournament game as a freshman basketball player. As a result, and to top it all off, the coach was very angry and benched him for the first half of the game. This all happened because he could not live or perform without insulin and no one would give him a break.

Fortunately, for Eric, five games later he became a starter and freshman All-Conference player. It is hard to ignore commitment to succeed driven by a desire to prove others wrong. This is the kind of inequity that can be experienced by a young person with diabetes.

Holidays are always incredible family gatherings highlighted by tons of love, laughter, and gratitude. Great grandmas, Grandmas, grandpa, aunts, uncles, and cousins are a constant part of our kingdom and when we are all together everything is right with the world! Christmas is a favorite time of our year and getting Eric home then was like icing on the cake. With his basketball commitment, he needed to return to school on December 27th. We had a fantastic few days but when he drove back in the winter storm, somewhere along the way, he started feeling sick. He had come down with the flu. The campus was closed down for the holiday, but his dorm was open for the returning ball players. A huge dormitory filled with nothing but empty rooms and he was going there to be sick on the top floor with not even an elevator or anyone to check in on him. But then I learned he was not the only occupant in his dorm. One of his teammates was right down the hall. That helps. Most of the campus was vacant though, and there was no food service available. The setting I was forced to think about was my type 1 diabetic son, sick with the flu in his little, old dorm room on the fourth floor with no elevators, mostly by himself, without easy access to food, or drinks and no one to call who might serve as a temporary caregiver. In my mind all I could imagine was this was a story destined for a bad ending.

Good old technology became my closest ally and once again won major points with me. Thank God for cell phones. I had to ask the questions racing through my mind, "Before retiring to his room would he stock up on carbs, sugar juice, and quick fix munchies?" I asked him and he did stop at a store so he would be prepared, just in case he had a need for anything. Luckily, he has a refrigerator in his room to store his insulin and now his life support nourishments. I checked off one item from my long "mom" list of concerns. Next, I wondered if he fell asleep, would he wake up to check his blood sugar before it got dangerously low? I suggested he put his phone on the highest ring setting so it would "for sure" wake him up. He did that and one more check went on my list. It was bedtime, and with a quick reminder to check his blood sugar and eat something before he fell asleep, we said goodnight. With that he promised to call in the morning. He would see how he felt before deciding if he could go to practice.

Practice was at 10:00 so we waited for the call. When no call came I needed to speak to him – because I am scared and worried and now as I think a bit more, I am borderline paranoid. There was no answer after many tries. Was he still sleeping? Was he unconscious in bed? Was he comatose? Had he died? All these horrific questions kept twirling around in my head. He said he would call. There has to be something wrong. I am four hours away and feeling so helpless. My heart was racing and I started feeling nauseous. Then I remembered the Health Center had information on his condition. I called there immediately only to learn it was closed. What about security? They have to stay open, don't they?

I called and the guard agreed to take on the mission I had devised. He didn't know Eric from Adam, so I asked he go to the gymnasium equipped with a basketball roster. He could print it from the online roster and then he could go the gymnasium to spot him. Then I begged him to do some basic detective work. If he did not see him at practice, he would go to Eric's room and check on him. He said he would call as soon as possible with the facts (I thought it best to keep it secret from Eric because he would hate all of my fuss). I calmed my fears and refused to think the worst. Yet, I waited, and not so patiently for the detective (security) to call. He called and said Eric was at practice. I heaved a long thankful sigh to this "guardian angel" that had befriended both Eric and I. This may seem like goofiness but it is scary stuff in the life of the mother of a son with diabetes.

Campus life was always busy and full of so much commotion. There were always many decisions to make. Should I do this or that? Would it be a good choice or not? We encouraged Eric to wear a diabetes bracelet or necklace. He had no problem wearing a Livestrong or WWJD bracelet. Why not a diabetes rubber type bracelet? He never wanted to bring attention to himself because of the disease. He thought wearing a bracelet to advertise his problem wasn't part of the plan. What if he was having a dangerous insulin reaction? On the college campus they may brush it off as a drunken stupor. The results are similar and without some type of ID they wouldn't have any idea of how to treat the episode. A witness without any prior knowledge of Eric's condition would probably snicker, get him into a cold shower, or serve him a hot cup of coffee and some aspirin. A small and simple misconception of this complication could cost him his life. It is hard for anyone and especially the general public to distinguish between an unconscious diabetic and an unconscious drunk. This is a constant issue and I certainly hope and wish somehow we can find a way to clarify diagnosis. For now Eric will live with the risk. And I will suffer the worry. Once again – it is out of my hands and it is in His.

Eric had lots of success during his freshman year while playing for the Hamline Pipers basketball team. He was twice named MIAC Player of the Week. He was responsible for leading many runs that accounted for come from behind wins. Some weeks he would score over 30 points in multiple games. He scored 40 in one game. He was at the top of the entire conference in several individual categories. The athletics dream was coming true. He received a number of accolades that are unusual to freshman players for his talent. He made the All-Conference Freshman team for the MIAC conference. His coach kept telling him that someday he would be an All American basketball player.

All of the success did not come without challenges. As he was tearing up the conference it seemed other teams were trying to figure out how to stop him and when nothing else worked they began to play extremely physical defense. Shortly after Christmas he got chopped at the knees by a short defender and dislocated his knee. He sat only two games and then came back to score 21. Eight games later, having scored ten points in the first eight minutes of play, he drove to the basket and four opposing players hammered him with a guard chopping down hard across his nose and cheekbones. He went to the ground but jumped up shaking his head. When the official presented the ball to Eric to shoot his free throws he saw his nose was pushed off to one side. He allowed Eric to shoot the free throws and then called time-out. He left the game but plugged the nose with gauze and went in to play another four minutes before he decided he was too beat up to play safely. He had surgery the next Thursday and they repaired the broken nose and fractured cheekbones. He played the remainder of the season with a mask. Aside from these challenges he enjoyed college life and worked hard to balance academics, athletics, and his social life all around his diabetes and the physical demands of being a college athlete.

There was a sense of knowing the ropes as Eric returned for his sophomore year. He was ready to live off campus. He had arranged to live with a couple buddies. We were all anxious to see his new place. On the outside it looked like a nice old house but inside it was awful. We learned it had been condemned, was in need of many repairs, but they were being scheduled to occur over the next 30 days. Eric's bedroom was located upstairs and as we walked up the skinny, rickety stairway we all were having second thoughts about the place. Steve tore the door case off in order to get his bed up and we moved things in successfully but I could not get comfortable. As I looked at the room I kept thinking that Eric is nearly 6' 6" tall and there is no way he can fit out through the bedroom window if there was a fire or any other disaster forcing him to escape quickly. How would anyone find him or treat him if he had an insulin reaction? After being responsible for his well-being for all of these years how could we leave him there?

Steve called the landlord the next week and was very unimpressed with him. When he followed up with the city housing office he was even less impressed. It was an impossible situation. Eric got out of his contract, but not without lots of headaches and costs. Where would he live now as school was starting in less than a week? He moved in to live with some of the basketball guys – slept on the couch – until he could find another option. Coincidently, one of his teammate's and temporary roommate's brother had just bought a new home and he was looking for a roommate to help with rent. It was about ten miles from campus, but at this time there are not a lot of choices. Had his and my good roommate luck run out? Think again. His new roommate just happened to be a young policeman. Thank you God now for about the trillionth time! Eric would be living with a police officer who is trained in emergencies of all kinds, including medical assistance to diabetics. He said out on his beat it was a common occurrence. Bingo, I feel like we have won the jackpot.

Basketball is a major passion for Eric, but during the next couple of years huge physical disappointments and medical expenses took their toll on all of us. A broken leg, broken nose, broken knee, crazy coaches, but never a broken spirit. His career may have ended early because of diabetes because patella tendinosis which usually heals with adequate rest and recovery has never healed and so we will never know how good this amazing athlete could have been in the full blooming years of his college sports career. Being raised as a diabetic gave him extra strength and determination needed to overcome hard times, to deal with obstacles, and to live every day to the fullest and in a kind, disciplined, and respectful manner. That's how diabetics must live or they will be relying on luck to live a long and happy life. Eric is not a guy to take chances, or to rely on luck, especially with his health and happiness.

Eric's successful and healthy lifestyle habits are admired by people he does not even know. As a result of his efforts and discipline he was invited to speak to diabetes focus groups made up of physicians, nurses, diabetic coaches, and pharmaceutical sales people. His first speaking engagement required him to introduce himself and then a panel was designated to serve him questions designed to educate the professionals in attendance. Eric regards it as easy money coming from easy answers because he is addressing his life, his practices, his experiences, and all of the information is firsthand knowledge from him. It's about his life as a diabetic. He is an accomplished athlete, on the University of St, Thomas NCAA III National Championship Team. He is a fun and friendly young man who is also very kind and open to helping others. He has lived the illness for nearly twenty years. What could be easier and more informative than that? If they only knew-well I guess they are getting to know. This is a blessing for me to see he is so willing to share and deliver a message about his life that is inspirational to the professionals who lead action and change in treatment of his illness. It is the greatest and most heroic gift to be given to his fairy Godmother. It is as though he has granted me my first wish.

As Joran finished high school I am much more relaxed and comfortable with sending him off to college. Is it that way for each child as they graduate? We have learned from the many challenges all of us have learned from Eric and for that reason the challenging stories about Joran's transition to college are not nearly as long. When we have multiple children we must remember to rejoice equally in each of their successes. They are certainly no less but they are experienced differently and so I rejoice differently. This experience is a personal revelation to me. Joran graduated with high honors as the salutatorian of his class. He was ranked number one in his class of 600 when we moved to our new home and he remained true to himself and his passion for educational excellence. He was honored to be allowed to deliver one of the commencement speeches. In that speech he encouraged, and challenged his fellow classmates to go into the world with energy and the common goal to follow their dreams. He demanded they give their best in everything they do and to never give up their dreams.....

"If I would have let the fear of change hold me back, I would've missed out on a great part of my life. So graduates, as you take the next step of your life, whatever that may be, don't let fear hold you back! I know that all of you have dreams, even if some of you don't, believe you can achieve them. I expect, and hope that each and every one of you will go out of these doors and chase your dreams. Because nothing is stopping you! The book "The Dream Giver" stated it best by saying, "Your horizon is full of promise. Another big dream is out there waiting for you, and if you don't pursue it, something important won't happen.""

You meet with fears and obstacles, but stay positive and your dreams will come true. I had heard this somewhere before, and then it came clear, that's what we always tell and portray through our actions to our children as they are growing up. Joran got it. This is how Joran lives and will continue to live. I was so proud and full of hope for the future that day I can still feel it now nearly three years later. All of the sadness, doubt, and questions I have been living through every day of his "life with diabetes" are gone and they are replaced by joy, hope, and confidence that his will be a truly successful future no matter where or what he does. His happiness will come from what lies in his heart and that has been given by the grace of God. My second wish has come true.

When Joran was a young boy, and newly diagnosed with diabetes he expressed his calling to do something big in his life. He had vowed to dedicate his life to become a better caregiver than the ones he knew for diabetics and his ultimate mission will be to find a cure, not talk about it. He would do his purpose for three people in his immediate world and as importantly for millions of people around the globe. He constantly worked very hard in school to excel, and was always disciplined to learn as much as he could about everything. He was invited by the baseball team to pitch and at the same time he is honored with scholarships to study biology in the pre-med program at Augustana College. He is on his Division II baseball team despite a major reconstructive shoulder surgery and rehab that most pitchers cannot recover from. He has learned to overcome and we are sure that he will. He has been a champion many times in sports and life and his future is bright with the same angel dust that has been spread throughout our lives. It is unreal how easy it is to forget lows when the highs are so big. He is capable of anything, just as he encouraged his friends and classmates and now I know he will balance his exciting new life amazingly well. He too will be a strong, thoughtful, disciplined leader like we so desperately need in this world filled with inconsistency and failed discipline. Thank you God for the blessings you are granting us through our children.

Eric and Joran are both now on new adventures. They are learning to love life and grow in their independence and masculinity. They are completely capable and confident in living with their diabetes. They will never let it be a limitation to anything they want to do or be. I have been the protagonist, the supporter, the advocate, and champion of that cause. Even though I was scared and frustrated at times by opposing fears and forces I always tried to accomplish the

"Big Dream" of being the best mom I could be. That is my life mission, goal, and profession and today I feel I have banked millions and millions of dollars' worth of joy. There is no bank account, credit rating, new cars, boats, multi-million dollar homes, or extravagant vacations to book as a result of my work but come on ..... every one of those things is temporary. This achievement of being a parent is a full time job that delivers more value than anything else on earth because it gives back for eternity. I am the fairy godmother. I have sprinkled magic dust along the way and I have broken the wicked spells that have so unrighteously been cast on our castle. The dust I have shared is through words, acts, emotions, and grace. I did not make them, but instead I have helped them, along with my entire family, to live their happily-ever-after lives.

Eric and Joran have now become the central characters of their own illustrious stories. They are the focus of their own themes, schemes, accidents, and incidences of life and it is their responsibility to engage the world's interest and enthusiasm. They will need to learn to walk confidently across the bridge owned by the nasty troll. They will act as Snow White did, and not be naïve in trusting all strangers. They will need to cross the thorn forest to safely reach their destination. With their own strength and aggression they will face the Big Bad Wolf and I know that they will defeat him easily. There is nothing these boys cannot do. The song, "You Raise Me Up" by Josh Groban expresses my feelings very well.

You raise me up, so I can stand on mountains;
You raise me up, to walk on stormy seas;
I am strong, when I am on your shoulders;
You raise me up... To more than I can be.

Like all of us, they will be slowed by opposing forces and they will learn the necessary lessons. Yet, no matter what their futures hold, it will be determined for them – not by them. That is the blessing God has given all of us.'

Chapter Twenty Four

We have encountered a lot of "good fairies" in our family, but no one defined the title more clearly than their grandmas and grandpas. They have all performed "legendary deeds." All of them have left our simple, little world and moved to the great land of eternity. We know, even from Heaven, they continue to guide and support us by sprinkling their magic dust along our path. Their acts of kindness, love, teaching, have enabled us to successfully survive the challenges of diabetes and to raise powerful, and positive young men. These are a few of the stories that will live forever in our hearts.

Grandpa Charles went to the heavenly bench first. Eric and grandpa had a very special connection that sadly lasted only two short years. When Eric was born it was as though something magical grew between he and his grandpa. There was an unusual and uncanny connection. Eric and Grandpa both had big, bright, sparkling blue eyes and when they connected they ignited a spark that had a magical power to forever unite their souls. They were inseparable. Charles was a retired superintendent, high school basketball coach, and founder of a great legion baseball program in his hometown. He was a constant playmate, and wise and gentle mentor. In Eric's eyes, along with most other people's, Grandpa could do no wrong. Grandpa was never too busy to spend time with Eric. He pitched to Eric. He rebounded for Eric. He ran routes and caught football passes from Eric. Even less than ten hours before he suddenly died of a heart attack, he was in the back yard energetically playing with his grandson. Eric was with Grandpa up until the unexpected end. The spark had no signs of burning out as they were together. They spent a last beautiful fall afternoon raking leaves, sharing a fire with toasted marshmallows, and playing football. Eric was spending the weekend alone with his grandma and grandpa and loving every minute. The amazing thing about this story is Eric was only two and a half years old and already had a mature and grounded relationship already when his grandpa died.

The last night with Grandpa they relaxed together playing games in the living room and then they both went to bed. The next morning Grandpa got up early to be ready for another exciting day and while combing his hair he realized something was wrong and went to tell Grandma Delores he needed help. Just like that, the world changed and a sudden heart attack stole the great man from our arms. Eric never woke. Despite the fact of ambulances, EMT's trying to revive him, and then the tears and disbelief of Grandma in response to this astonishing loss. Eric's sound and peaceful sleep was another great blessing and perhaps he was there holding Grandpa's hand as he left earth and transitioned through the Heavenly gates. When Eric awoke he was greeted with great love by Grandma. Her 30+ years of teaching came clearly to the surface as she dealt with her loss and sadness and then as she explained the love of both of their lives was gone. Her kind, caring, passionate, broken-hearted, and yet, simple, loving words came flowing out as she said "Grandpa's heart stopped working this morning and he has gone to Heaven."

With confusion, and sweet and simple innocence Eric went to the large bay windows to look outside, with his eyes seeking grandpa working on his leaves out there in spite of grandma's crazy talk. When he turned around, his eyes were filled with the spark of knowing, excitement, and confidence as he said "No, he's not gone Grandma, his truck is right there in the driveway and grandpa could not leave without his truck." He then started to search around the house for Grandpa and so Grandma had to reassure him Grandpa had gone. Those moments, and that exchange of love, closeness, and support they shared during that most difficult time, formed a bond that never wavered through the last twenty years of her life. Just as his truck remained in the driveway, so does the magical spark that grew from his grandpa's spirit remain in Eric's person to this day. Grandpa Charles died too soon to directly influence any of our other children but through Eric and Grandma his values, personality, and love did influence our family for future generations. He is, I am sure, so proud of them all as he looks down upon all of us. He was spared from learning Eric is diabetic, just like Steve. It was approximately a year from Grandpa's passing that Eric became a type 1 diabetic. I know Grandpa would have struggled greatly with this news, and so once again, God works in His own miraculous ways.

My personal fairy godmother and another "good fairy" to all of our children was my mom. As you remember, she granted a magic wish of mine as Eric's special caregiver. She made it possible to complete my commitment to teach and at the same time to learn the value, importance, and joy I would have as a full time mom. Her bag of "fairy dust" never ran low. She was a ball of positive energy for all of us. Her personality was electrifying, and she did everything to make every moment we had with her a memory that would last a lifetime. She dealt the magic cards that kept uncles and aunts, brothers, sisters, and cousins excited to be there, to care, and to share. It was important and essential every success and special moment was recognized and celebrated with enthusiasm and love. She celebrated much in her life and was thankful for all of the joy her grandchildren brought to her. She was a shining lamp of laughter, unity, and love that burned brightly and still burns brightly in all our lives. Grandmas can be forever if they want to be and that is a privilege of positive parenting. Her spirit will live in our presence for as long as we all live and breathe.

Just as her light sparked so vibrant and bright, it was suddenly, that the light of my life burned dim. This tiny in stature, huge in character, beautiful lady with her hair as white as snow and lips as red as a new rose suddenly became very ill. Even though she was beautiful both inside and out there was something ugly in her physical self. Reminiscent of the classic tale "Snow White" just when everything seemed to be going perfectly, Grandma's illness came and grew fast and unstoppable. It was as though a wrinkled, old, peddler arrived on Grandma's step and offered a rosy, but poisonous apple. She never dreamed of what was coming....pancreatic cancer. The sickness is like taking more than a bite out of a poison apple. It is like drinking from the bottle of poison. Grandma innocently lost her energy, joy, and one hundred mile hour attitude and fell into a deep pit that was dark, dreary, filled with sadness and evil. What she thought was just a tender stomach that was bothered by the wrong foods was really the indicator of the foe that would end her life so harshly and cruelly. Oh, Lord, why does evil so quietly and suddenly slip into our lives when it would seem goodness should result from doing good in the world?

We all tried to break this evil spell. We prayed and we believed she would win. We told her it would be fixed and she would feel good again. Yet, chemotherapies, surgeries, infections, and then a decision not to be kept alive became a walk through the valley of the shadow of death for all of her children. She quickly became too weak to move by herself and then she laid for months with us all at her side. Maybe the handsome prince's kiss could wake her? Would our declining Grandpa, in the midst of debilitating failure from Parkinson's disease deliver the energy to heal from his unwavering fifty-one years of love? No, that is not possible, as a matter of fact Grandpa had been living with Parkinson's disease for years with Grandma at his front side and fighting many of his battles, without any of us even knowing. As forty-year-old adults three of us children (my two brothers and I) could not keep up the demanding requirements of caring for him and his disease when she was unable to. Once again, the energy, power, and will of Grandma was proven greater than any of us could imagine.

As I stated, my mom had incredible energy and passion. She entered her battle with this cancer, determined to fight the terrible disease all the way to her last breath. I watched her fight without food or drink for nearly a month. I watched her never give up. I watched her become nothing but a shell. Our family learned together that our body is only a harbor for our spirit when we touched her physically and at the same time knew her spirit had already gone to another place. As I watched her eyes close for the last time, mine opened wider than ever before. She had taught me the most valuable life lessons. She taught me love and commitment. She taught me joy and excitement. She taught me how to laugh and cry. She held me so closely in her arms and in her heart I will never lose the feeling. She taught me to fight for what is right with extraordinary emotional and powerful faith. She knew she was going to Heaven. Yet, the love she had for her family and times she wanted to share kept her living when it was not even really possible to live. In the later days, the fellowship and prayers we all shared together were priceless. I learned how to die gracefully. I became aware that the love of a good family is the greatest gift one could ever be given. And at the same time I learned I should speak my feelings and express my thoughts clearly each day. When she was gone I still had not heard some of the things that I so wanted to hear. What does life mean? How does life look at its end? What is the most important achievement I can accomplish in life? Who can I trust? How much did I please her and did I give her what she needed as she gave what was needed to me? The wisdom she shared is another expected but unusual blessing because so much of the wisdom came not from what was said or done but by what was left behind. Those blessings will continue to grow in each day of my life because of the way she taught them to me.

Grandpa followed Grandma only three months later. The big strong, loving, Christian man who was an exceptional athlete, intelligent businessman, and family leader could not stand, speak, smile, or laugh anymore. His ending came because complications of the illness are greater than the minds that work to eliminate them. He was taken by another disastrous ending to a good, good, life. He was given up to die, quietly, and peacefully. My mom and dad were good people and they struck out on devastating curve balls. How they swung was more important than when they struck out. They were a wonderful example of love and care to all of us. They taught all of us to live life every day. They taught me a good example never ends. They taught me family means teamwork. As in the "Three Musketeers" – "All for one and one for all." Each day brings its own unique lessons, joys, sadness, and happy moments. My entire family and I miss them every day but draw comfort in knowing we live with their spirit in our hearts while they are in heaven, celebrating God's joyful eternity together.

In spite of the fact I was nearly fifty years-old when my parents died, I began to feel how lonely it must feel to be an orphan. I remember clearly how we shared and they cared about everything. Now I would never feel that love again. It was an amazingly lonely feeling and a feeling I didn't like dwelling on for long. I had to remind myself regularly that now I have an additional responsibility as both a parent and a grandparent. To the last minute I was their daughter, and I needed my mom and dad with me to make me feel full and right. Today, I am the mom and I am in charge. This is the changing of the guards. Loss of parents has given me a new inner strength and independence I am growing into and learning to live with. It is empowering me, and it is quite impossible to explain. My mom is living through me and in me. I truly can feel her presence and I feel more whole than I ever have before.

I sometimes find myself thinking about my parents' painful deaths. Would I die in that same terrible way? Do I have to suffer with worry about pancreatic cancer or

Parkinson's disease? I cancelled my check-ups and decided I would put them on hold for a while. I am scared and began to question the legitimacy of my own exceptional health. My own mortality had never been a real consideration for me. Through the loss I know my mother never prepared for the end of her life because one day she was a caregiver for my dad, her own mom, and anyone else who needed help and then suddenly she was too sick to think about anything but survival. I never got a chance to ask her if that was all right. I wondered if it is the best way to live. I just cannot deal with any more disappointing news, especially if it is about me. Life isn't fair...and so who do I trust and what do I trust in. I am mom and there are a lot of people counting on me to be here and I am not going to let them down, so help me God.

I shared my insecurity and feelings of fear with Steve. He has lived nearly every day of his life with so much gusto and confidence. Where does that come from? He simply told me that he was forced to face his mortality at a very young age. Diabetes had enabled-forced him to do that. He learned to believe he lives on God's terms and he enjoys each day by doing all he can. He claims that to give +100% at all times means you do not have to wonder if you have done enough. He says you need to do things for fun and with fun as your purpose. He expresses gratitude for every complex or simple obstacle or opportunity, success or failure. He recognizes and praises God in the presence of anyone he meets. He told me to know that no matter what I expect, want, or need I am not in charge. It will all happen according to God's plan. He then pointed out another reminder I have on my wall that says, "May you trust God that you are exactly where you are meant to be." He told me if you truly believe in God and believe you are living His plan and give Him your heart and mind to do with as He pleases, then when or how you die is not within your control and it is not important. No one knows when their last day will come. He quoted Psalm 118:24 "This is the day that the LORD has made; let us rejoice and be glad in it." Why worry? Steve always has an uncanny and thorough way of getting me back in tune and on course. That is another blessed lesson from diabetes. Life is ours to live on God's terms and in God's time. It is up to us to make the most of it.

Both Eric and Joran also have this magical or mystical way of looking at mortality. They live joyfully and confidently each day with the faith that God is watching over them. Living with a chronic disease, they look at life differently than most of us. They don't sweat over the small or big stuff. They just seem to have grown up faster and have reached maturity a little faster than other kids. They probably have considered the complications that can come with diabetes and have decided those worries are not worth their energy. They seem to have sorted out their feelings and come to grips with mortality earlier than most other people because they are forced to. I believe that they are wise beyond their years. I also believe now, they have it right. I have begun to live with the same openness and confidence and it feels so good. I am living God's plan and not mine. I am watching and waiting for His guidance in my days and nights. I can tell anyone, anytime and in any way I am guided by Him and believe that all that I am and will be is because He is taking me there. What a blessing! 2 Corinthians 4:6 says it best, "For God, who commanded the light to shine out of darkness, has shined in our hearts, to give the light of the knowledge of the glory of God in the face of Jesus Christ."

All three of my men with diabetes have taught me about living life to the fullest. They do not worry about silly stuff. When I begin feeling sorry for myself I stop, and think about all of them, and others with similar challenges. It is through this reflection I can return to the right track, the track of faith and love. Their way and their stories give me the strength I need. In the fairy tale world, their life is like

Rapunzel's hair because they leave me memories to cling to when I need to climb the wall to find peace in life. I can act and think with the confidence and gusto I have experienced with them. I am unusually privileged and blessed to share my life and to learn to live with my very wise husband and sons. They constantly and consistently teach and remind me how to live life to its fullest measure.

Chapter Twenty Five

As one sibling moves to college and the next steps up confidently to lead, the dynamics in our home continue to change. From Eric to Joran, from Joran to Greg, and now from Greg to Chad the new head honchos assume and live up to their own unique and brand new responsibilities as leaders. Each becomes an example for the younger sibling(s). It is fun to see how each of our sons and daughter evolve with time. I feel as though the maturity and approach to life permeate all of them with equal sincerity. Yet, they are all unique. The oldest is at all times in control and even tempered. Not much gets him high and not too much gets him low. He is the rock. The second is so serious and driven to be responsible and successful. He is articulate, mature, extremely driven to be self-sufficient and at the same time as respectful loving and constant in all situations. The third is our communicator, our joker, and yet he is too intelligent and smart for his own good. He can get A's without studying or worrying. The fourth is street smart and capable of doing anything he puts his mind to. He has always been an over achiever and must be challenged and rewarded for accomplishment in order to stay at the top of his game and exceed all expectations. The fifth and only girl in the mix has a sweetness that is truly incomparable and honest. She is the finest mix of all of the unique flavors that surround her. She is the connector, through her sincere love, passion, and joy for each of her brothers and all that they say and do. All of our family are constant in their love and connection to each other and they are all influenced by each other and comfortably live in each other's worlds. They are all champions in their ways and values. The changing of the guard is happening about every two years three times now like clockwork. Chad has now moved into the driver's seat. It is he who has felt the loneliness most with the loss of all of his older brothers. It would not be so hard if they did not live life as though all of them were part of the others but that is not the case. These siblings are all 100% into the activities, thoughts, successes, failures, values and goals of each other. No one goes anywhere alone, no matter how far from home. Chad is finding comfort in his new rank in our kingdom not only as the lone knight but also as the emotional guide and example for his sister. He is also learning to integrate directly with his old parents on his own terms and in his own way.

Magic continues to weave its way through our lives. Personal power is what magic is all about. Taking charge of your own life is the lesson being learned. Much has happened in the kingdom as the hours, weeks, months, years and decades have flown by. Silvia Hartmann says, "The world needs individuals who are creative, who contribute, who serve and who role model lives of splendid joy, satisfaction and achievement for the younger generation." The "good fairy" who taught us all about this was Grandma Delores. She just recently left this earth and our world on some very sad and disappointing terms. We learned in her death the sad results when people do not act in the best interest or with sincere compassion and concern for people who trust and believe in them.

Grandma has always been very conscientious with her health and wellness. If she felt poorly enough to be concerned she would get to her doctor immediately. She was 83 years old and very strong and healthy – a city commissioner, district political party chairman, advocate for community development, piano teacher, church organist, you name it. One day she felt as though she had a case of bronchitis coming and drove to the emergency room to check in. They gave her shots and meds and sent her home telling her she would be fine and when she said she was concerned that it might get worse fast and she would like to stay rather than drive +100 miles by herself each time to get checked out they told her they could not admit her due to new healthcare regulations.

She went home in a very sick condition and waited for the meds to work as promised within 24 hours. When this did not happen she drove the 50 miles again and rather than admit her when she could not walk into the pharmacy to pick up additional meds (they brought them out to her car) they still neglected to place her in the hospital. She went home to wait for the meds to beat her illness and in the meantime the very treatable illness began to get worse. The night after she drove +100 miles for the second time to find help for her sickness and was sent home she was rushed in by ambulance to a different hospital and died of pneumonia. This loss again has hurt very deeply and seems so unjust. She was our rock and passed away for no reconcilable reason other than negligence. Every day she was alive she taught us all through both her words and her deeds without magic the world is fruitless, life is meaningless, and difficulty is hard and painful. Because she believed in the magic of living life to its fullest her every day was always filled with grandeur. She had meaning right through her last day and she experienced no difficulty even in her death …they say she died with a smile on her lips.

We all miss her every day but her spirit stays with us and I have proof as I watch my daughter and witness her love, care, concern, and amazing confidence. When she asked if she could sing "This Little Light of Mine" at Grandma's celebration service I realized life does go on. Grandma's spark lived in the beautiful way my little princess sang and also in the way that she lives every day. Her personality is so unique in the way she presents her sincerity and in how she truly cares about everyone she meets.

Kyrsten also carries a very high level care and responsibility for her daddy since Grandma has passed. She was with him in the country, emptying a truck filled with Grandma's things while clearing out her house for the last time when his blood sugar dropped and there was nothing to give him to fix the problem. She, her best friend, and Chad were alone in the country dumping and burning garbage five miles away from the nearest human beings. They all got very scared when Steve became relatively senseless and without any prompt access to another adult the kids called me and kept him safe by taking the car keys. Once again, I know the blessing of the cell phone. They did all of the right things to help fix the problem but she must have made a pledge to herself to never let it happen again. She is very maternal and careful when going anywhere with her dad. She prepares and is ready with sweets to prevent any possible problem. It is kind of like Grandma is right there helping and guiding her every step of the way.

Delores was my mentor in caring for and living with diabetics in my household. She was my beloved friend as a virtuoso in the art of living graciously with the disease of diabetes. For every one of my sons and daughter she was the trusted friend and knowledgeable advocate who had the right attitude, ideas, and approach to achieve success. We learned to live every moment you have with your parents, grandparents, and all other seniors you are blessed to experience to the fullest. Let them talk with you and to you because you want to listen and you will learn a lot about life. It will be well worth your time.

Chapter Twenty Six

At the beginning of my story I desperately desired to live my life as a real life fairy godmother with the power of spreading magic dust throughout our kingdom. I was on a mission to break the evil spell that had been put on my husband and two young sons. My wish was to conquer the wicked challenges associated with the illness of diabetes so these special individuals would all live happily ever after lives. I still wish for this, but now I know real magic comes through making choices and enjoying each moment as we walk day by day into our very own future. My experiences have taught me much about appreciation and respect. Ultimately, no matter how I try to figure it out or break it down the answer always comes up I am where I am supposed to be and I will go where I am supposed to go. No matter how important, strong, determined, smart, or driven I am - nothing happens if it is not part of my plan, the plan, His plan for me. It is this lesson that seems universally true and has the power to deliver peace and understanding to all of us. Philippians 4:7 "And the peace of God, which surpasses all understanding, will guard your hearts and your minds in Christ Jesus." I am saved by this knowledge and if you take the time to think about it and realize it you may be too.

As I have lived, loved, laughed, and cried through life I still marvel at the wisdom of my favorite fairy tales. The wisdom they so simply illustrate is incredible. They always place strong importance on Christian ideas, such as the preservation of the family unit. The number three is significant in fairy tales because it stands symbolic for a family. Three conveys a message of relevance and in my world the threes happened over and over again. Three diabetics, three living grandparents - Three different homes - Three tries at having a little girl. It was not a single occurrence, or just happening twice by coincidence. It seems things often happen in threes. My experiences with three are sufficient and significant enough to help me realize when there are three I do not ask which one. I cannot ignore any because I cannot separate them equally. I also cannot focus on one and ignore the other because I cannot pick between them. This significance dates back a long way. In most religions, it is a special and holy number. In the Christian faith you have the Holy Trinity. These are our angels of faith, hope, and love. As a family with three diabetics we succeed in all dimensions. My family has changed our little part of the world not intentionally but unintentionally by sharing our time, resources, disciplines, happiness, joy, faith and love. I get it God!

Symbols do not happen by chance in fairy tales and it is likely they do not happen by chance in life. Their presence is symbolic. Recognition of them in our real lives means we are thoughtful of the world we live in. Symbolism strikes at my heart in many ways and shapes. Three very special people in my world had been given diabetes. None of them had it any better or worse than anyone else. The disease is only a small part of who they are but it is also an influence on who they are in a very big way. Being a person with diabetes does not mean they are sickly and need more of my attention than anyone else. Living healthy is not just the absence of sickness. Good health is vitality, vigor, high energy, emotional and mental clarity, and physical endurance. These are the gifts to pray for and these are the qualities that my guys all possess! They can do anything, be anything, and overcome anything while being fearless and disciplined according to the rules imposed on them by the "blessing /disease" they have been cursed or coerced by. The symbolic three means I could not select one as my favorite or another to ignore. They are all equally and uniquely loved and cared for just as our entire odd number of seven family members are cared for by each other equally and uniquely. This world of equal and unique love is another unusual blessing life has lead me to cherish. No matter what the circumstance, demand, trouble, or pain, ever since the moments my husband and children have been with me I have not felt any jealousy or dislike. I believe my once selfish, desirous, perfect world characteristics have been evolved so I now live to love. I am happy with this place because in John 13:34-35 Jesus says, "A new command I give you: Love one another. As I have loved you, so you must love one another. By this everyone will know that you are my disciples, if you love one another." And it is good.

The number seven is also a magic number in fairy tales. Seven is used for symbolism in many ways and places. Seven days in a week, seven continents, seven seas, and there are seven colors in the color wheel. Seven comes from the Bible, perhaps from adding three (the heavenly number) with four (which represents earth). Much of Jesus' word is in parables and is strewn with symbolism. Is my world a fairy tale? I think not, but I do believe it makes an interesting parable. If I believe in God's will and also that he takes me where I am supposed to be, then I know I have been righteously called to deliver this message to the world. We have three family members battling diabetes and there are four of us who have and always will be battling it with them. We are in this together, as a family, until the very end. We have all learned how to accomplish great things as a team. The list is endless and runs from Dean's lists, to national college basketball championships, to invention of one of the world's most innovative health technologies. Every day holds moments we share. We make the best of the worst and achieve the most with the least.

God somehow and for some reason seems to give me great challenges I never expected nor did I think I would be able to overcome. I have often wondered, why me? This can only be answered with faith because it is my path. The unusual result of every challenge though has been greater knowledge of myself, more comfort with the world I live in, a closer relationship with Him, and an ability to experience all things in the presence of His will and purpose. It is through all of the unusual circumstances of life He has chosen to give me the greatest blessings and those blessings I am now experiencing with great joy. I know we all face challenges as we travel through this journey called life, and some say how we handle the challenges is the real test. Today I would state it differently and say, "It is who you ask to help you handle the challenges", that is the real test. For me, the call is simple because I know all of my challenges are part of God's plan for me and if I pray to Him for answers they will be revealed.

I know by walking through the years in order to reach today I am able to move forward with more strength and vitality than ever before. I am building a natural momentum and energy to do greater things than I ever thought were possible. What a wonderful life. I only wish I could have realized it sooner. I have grown to know it was essential for me to forget the life I'd planned, so I can fully engage, appreciate, and live the life that was planned and has been waiting for me all along. God has helped me to reach this understanding through obstacles, opportunities, successes, failures, and a lot of trial and error. The command "Open Sesame" was memorized and lived in my heart since I was a young girl. I only wish I would have fully understood its power and had been more aware of its significance earlier in my life. God always had the plan and I just needed to jump on board in order to feel the joy of that significance. I needed to "let go" and "let God."

The journey of life can be a fairy tale adventure. However, as Mark Twain once said, "Fiction must be absolutely believable." This story is real and it is written to teach a lesson. My world and family are growing, changing, and thriving every day by celebrating daily, overcoming obstacles with humility and hard work, and in attacking opportunity like there is no tomorrow. It is fun and it is good. I have accepted that I am called - not that I am calling. As for diabetes, I must continue to be an advocate and champion of the cause to achieve a real cure – not a treatment. This story is filled with universal truth about real people in the real world. The reality I write about is filled with hope and promise that should be shared by all people in all places. I am very happy to say I have been "blessed with unusual happiness" in my life. I live my happily-ever-after days with a spiritual and magical belief that if you have faith, hope, and trust, along with a little pixie dust, your loveliest dreams really, truly can come true.

The End

Made in the USA
Charleston, SC
23 March 2013